Pulling Together

286.06   3744

Vestal.

Pulling

DATE D

286.06
CLASS

Vestal.
3744
ACC
(LAST NAME OF AUTHOR)

Pulling together.
(BOOK TITLE)

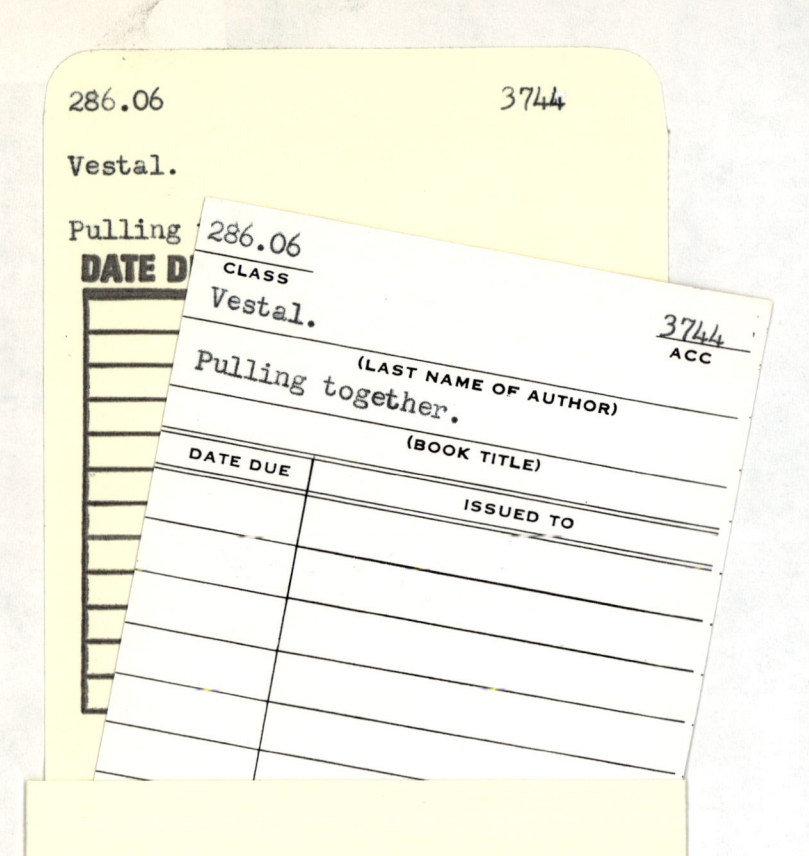

DATE DUE	ISSUED TO

First Baptist Church Library
Tomball, Texas

PULLING TOGETHER!

Daniel Vestal
Robert A. Baker

FIRST BAPTIST CHURCH LIBRARY
TOMBALL, TEXAS

BROADMAN PRESS
Nashville, Tennessee

© Copyright 1987 • Broadman Press
All rights reserved
4264-06
ISBN: 0-8054-6406-9
Dewey Decimal Classification: 286.06
Subject Heading: COOPERATIVE PROGRAM
Library of Congress Catalog Card Number: 87-18637
Printed in the United States of America

Unless otherwise noted, Scripture quotations are from the King James Version of the Bible. Scripture quotations marked (RSV) are from the Revised Standard Version of the Bible, copyrighted 1946, 1952, © 1971, 1973.

Vestal, Daniel, 1944–
   Pulling together!/Daniel Vestal, Robert A. Baker.
   p.   cm.
   ISBN 0-8054-6406-9
   1. Southern Baptist Convention—Missions.
   2. Baptists—Missions.
I. Baker, Robert Andrew. II. Title.
BV2520.V47   1987
266'.6132—dc19   87-18637
                                                        CIP

Contents

Introduction
William M. Pinson, Jr.
Part I: The History of the Cooperative Program
Robert A. Baker
1. The Biblical Call to World Missions   15
2. Baptists Facing the Challenge of World Missions   25
3. The Cooperative Program and World Missions   46
Part II: The Local Church and the Cooperative Program   Daniel G. Vestal, Jr.
4. The Church as a Base for World Mission   71
5. The Pastor as a Leader in World Missions   86
6. Cooperation as the Strategy for World Missions   103

Introduction
William M. Pinson, Jr.

This book, written by two of Baptists' most dedicated, gifted, godly leaders, can benefit pastors and churches tremendously. It can help a church be faithful to the teachings of God's Holy Word and open channels of blessings for millions. I pray you will not only read it but apply its contents to your life and church.

God's Word places a heavy responsibility on us for sharing the good news about Jesus Christ with a lost world. The Bible's mandate for God's people to be involved in missions, evangelism, education, and benevolence is disturbingly clear, but detailed instructions on how to carry out that mandate are noticeably scarce. Jesus promised that the Holy Spirit would guide and empower us as we carry out His commands and follow His way. So we move forward by faith that we will receive guidance on how to do what Jesus has told us to do.

Such has been the case with Southern Baptists. As we have tried to be faithful to God's Word, directing our efforts to missions, evangelism, education, and benevolence, we have been led to a method of support which enables us to serve effectively. We have realized that individual Christians alone cannot carry out God's missionary mandate; only by being a part of a church can a person adequately respond to God's instructions to go into all the world. Churches are a gift from God to make it possible for Christians to be faithful to His commands. We have also realized that a single church, regardless of size, alone cannot adequately carry out God's marching orders. Only by being a part of a fellowship of churches cooperating together can a church fulfill its responsibilities.

While affirming the necessity of cooperation, Southern Baptists have struggled with the nature of that cooperation. For years each Baptist institution, agency, or cause made its own appeal to churches for support. This plan was ineffective and inefficient. Some churches were seldom called upon for support and therefore had little participation; others had frequent appeals which disrupted the work and worship of the church. A great deal of money was spent raising money. Causes with appealing pleas and eloquent fund raisers prospered; others, perhaps more deserving, floundered.

Through prayer and dedication, growing out of a longing to do God's work better, Southern Baptists developed the Cooperative Program. I believe the Holy Spirit, true to Jesus' promise, directed the development.

The Cooperative Program protects the autonomy of the churches at the same time it provides a means of cooperation so that churches can be faithful to God's Word. It allows every church and every church member to support all Baptist efforts with little time or money required to gather the funds. It enables Baptists to concentrate on doing God's work rather than raising the money with which to do it. It provides coordination of efforts and public accounting for funds. It is not perfect, but compared to the system that proceeded it and to alternatives sometimes advocated to replace it, the Cooperative Program is clearly superior.

This book tells the story of the Southern Baptist Cooperative Program—the biblical basis on which it rests; the stirring story of its development by God centered, Bible believing, Christ loving, Holy Spirit directed persons; the marvelous way in which it functions; the amazing account of its impact on our world to God's glory.

Pulling Together is written by two persons who know the Bible, Baptist people, and the Cooperative Program intimately. Robert A. Baker, renowned Baptist historian, has spent his life serving our Lord among Southern Baptists. A sought-after preacher, master teacher, and gifted writer, he has touched literally millions through his ministry. A professor of church history at Southwestern Baptist Theological Seminary since 1942, he has written and contributed to a number of books on Baptist history. Second to none in his knowledge of Southern Baptists in the past as well as today, he is emminently qualified to tell the story of the development of the Cooperative Program.

Professor Baker's first chapter emphasizes that the Bible is not merely a book with a missionary message, but that it is a missionary message. Both the Old and the New Testaments point to the missionary imperative from God. Chapter one points out that missions reveals God's true nature and enables Christians to achieve life's highest fulfillment through Christian stewardship. In a most interesting way the chapter chronicles the ebb and flow of the missionary commitment of Christians through the ages.

The second chapter by Baker describes how Baptists have attempted to answer the biblical call to world missions. The introductory discussion points to the difficulties Baptists have experienced in the formation of structures to do mission work. The body of the chapter summarizes various approaches Baptists have taken and the strengths and weaknesses of each. The final part of the chapter describes the early efforts of Southern Baptists to organize for missions.

Chapter three by Baker tells how the climax of Southern Baptist efforts to answer the biblical call to world missions is found in the Cooperative Program. He indicates that the most significant step ever taken by Southern Baptists in the support of world missions was the formation of the Cooperation Program. He sets forth the spectacular advance of the Southern Baptist Convention following the development and adoption of the Cooperation Program. A significant feature of the chapter is a presentation of the various criticisms of the Cooperative Program and some suggestions for a response. The closing section of the chapter is devoted to spelling out the excellences of the Cooperative Program and its value to Southern Baptists.

Daniel G. Vestal also writes out of a rich heritage in Southern Baptist life. His father was a well-known and respected evangelist. Pastor Vestal has been deeply involved in evangelism and missions, having conducted over three hundred revivals in the United States and in countries around the world. However, his most significant contribution to missions has come as pastor of a church. He became pastor of the First Baptist Church of Midland, Texas, in May of 1976 and, building on a great mission heritage, led that church to be the largest dollar contributor to the Cooperative Program in the Southern Baptist Convention and one of the highest in percentage giving. He has led the church in a variety of mission endeavors, striving to saturate the entire church with a love and zeal for missions. The three chapters he has contributed to the book are written from the perspective of a pastor with a love for missions, endeavoring to lead a church to develop that same love.

The first chapter by Vestal focuses on the place of the pastor as a strategic leader in the world mission enterprise. Vestal points out that the pastor leads by the use of his pulpit in equipping laypersons for missions. He insists that it is out of mission minded preaching and strong lay involvement that a missionary church is developed and grown.

Vestal's second chapter declares that the local church is the front upon which the battle for world missions will be fought. It will either be won or lost, according to Vestal, as to whether or not local churches are developed into missionary giving, going and supporting churches. This chapter focuses upon involvement of a church in the world mission enterprise through lay participation and stewardship development.

The third chapter by Vestal highlights cooperation as a strategy for world evangelization. Vestal contends that pastors and churches must get a vision of the kingdom of God on earth and the role of the church in extending that kingdom. Out of such a vision cooperative missions will flourish. This chapter focuses upon the principles of cooperation and on a pattern for cooperation. Vestal shows how cooperative funding and cooperative praying go hand in hand. Out of his own experience, Vestal suggests solid, practical ways in which a pastor can help a church develop participation in the cooperative mission program of Baptists.

In addition to the two authors, others have contributed significantly to the volume. Robert F. Polk, director, Cooperative Program Promotion for the Baptist General Convention of Texas, Edward Schmeltekopf, associate executive director of the Baptist General Convention of Texas, the staff of the Stewardship Commission of the Southern Baptist Convention, and the staff of Broadman Press of the Baptist Sunday School Board have all helped make the book possible.

Along with many other persons, I have experienced firsthand the marvelous benefits of the Cooperative Program. My own life has been molded by the ministries made possible through the Cooperative Program. I know that it works. On foreign, home, and state mission fields, in Baptist schools and benevolent institutions, in churches and through a multitude of programs to help Baptists effectively share the gospel I have seen the blessings the Cooperative Program brings.

I long for every Baptist to know what the Cooperative Program does, how it works, what it means. As our Baptist people are more and more informed I believe that they will more and more support the manifold ministries made possible through the Cooperative Program. I anguish over the number of needs unmet because of lack of support. I rejoice when I contemplate what will be done as Baptists increase their participation through the Cooperative Program.

I pray that this book will help every reader to become an advocate of the Cooperative Program. And I pray that every church which is part of our cooperating Baptist family will give regularly through the Cooperative Program. The future is bright for Baptists because of God's guidance and power, because of His gift to us of cooperative missions, because of His leading us to embrace the Cooperative Program as a major means of carrying out His Word. I thank God to be part of such a family of believers.

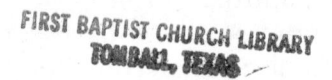

Part I
The History of the Cooperative Program
Robert A. Baker

1
The Biblical Call to World Missions

The chapel of Southwestern Baptist Theological Seminary was crowded one day in the spring of 1940 when Dr. Baker James Cauthen related his call to become a missionary in China. At the seminary this kind of personal testimony was the custom for newly appointed missionaries. Dr. Cauthen was professor of missions at the seminary and a rising young scholar. He was also pastor of a strong church in Fort Worth and was recognized as one of the outstanding speakers in the city. With simple and earnest words, he described how he had taught his students year after year about the great need for the gospel by the almost uncountable masses in China. At that very time, Japanese troops were mounting an offensive in a war with China. Dr. Cauthen revealed that his own heart was so overwhelmed by the call to minister to the people of China that he had resigned from his seminary professorship, had given up his good church, and with his lovely wife would soon leave his homeland for China.

As he neared the end of his testimony, Dr. Cauthen said, "Some of my friends have asked me if it was wise for me to leave the safety of Fort Worth to face the dangers of the bloody war in China. I told them that I would rather be in China amidst falling bombs in the will of God than to be in Fort Worth outside of His will."

Right there Dr. Cauthen put his finger on the dynamic for world missions: the will of God. He found the will of God by searching the inspired Scriptures and by heeding the leadership of the living Christ.

The Bible is a missionary book. Both the Old and the New Testaments teach that God wills for His people to be witnesses of His grace in all of the world. That is the essence of the definition of missions by Dr. W. O. Carver, one of the finest mission authors among Southern Baptists. He said, "Missions is the extensive realization of God's redemptive purpose in Christ through human instruments." This redemptive purpose of God is clearly revealed in the Old Testament. Dr. Carver wrote:

> We can never understand the Old Testament until we make our interpretation to turn upon the thought that the Hebrew people and literature were designed as a medium through which the universal God was approaching all His people throughout the human race.[1]

It is not possible for me in this brief study, of course, to give a detailed exposition of the Old Testament to demonstrate the correctness of Dr. Carver's statement. He has done that very thing in his two books *Missions in the Plan of the Ages* and *The Bible a Missionary Message* which are available in most Baptist libraries. I shall simply mention some of the key Old Testament Scriptures that teach of God's universal redemptive purpose. In Genesis 12:3, God said to Abraham that He would bless him, and that through "thee shall all families of the earth be blessed." Similarly, in Isaiah 49:6 God told Israel, "I will also give thee for a light to the Gentiles, that thou mayest be my salvation unto the end of the earth." In Isaiah 66:18, God said, "It shall come, that I will gather all nations and tongues; and they shall come, and see my glory." Both Jonah and Daniel are distinctly missionary in their outlook.

The New Testament is not only filled with the call to witness but was actually a product of the missionary enterprise. The missionary work of Paul provided the principal historical stem of the New Testament after the ascension of our Lord.

Paul's writings constantly emphasize the need for Christians to witness to all the world. Christians are to be ambassadors of Christ and laborers together with God. Paul emphasized also that the redemptive purpose of God was universal. In Romans 10:12-13, he wrote, "For there is no difference between the Jew and the Greek: for the same Lord over all is rich unto all that call upon him. For whosoever shall call upon the name of the Lord shall be saved."

The very nature of God's provision for sin shows that it was designed for all the world. That is what Paul meant in Romans 10:6-7 when he said that in order to be saved one is not required to ascend into heaven to bring a Savior down to the world nor to descend into the deep to bring up Christ from the dead. These things (the incarnation and the resurrection of Christ) were necessary for our salvation, yet no one was able to do them. But God has provided for the salvation of all humankind. Salvation is made available for all who confess with their mouths that Jesus Christ is Lord and believe in their hearts that God raised Him from the dead.

By this redemptive plan, God revealed His purpose to redeem humankind apart from the Jewish law, for "Christ is the end of the law for righteousness to every one that believeth" (Rom. 10:4). Because righteousness is God's free gift, no one can boast, claiming spiritual superiority. This righteousness comes from God, not from institutions or sacraments, priests or prelates or spiritual overlords. God's grace is found in Jesus Christ. As one writer has remarked, "The ground around the cross is completely level and wondrously smooth."

The four rhetorical questions Paul asked in Romans 10:14-15 define the Christian's part in God's plan. He stated in verse 13, "Whosoever shall call upon the name of the Lord shall be saved." The four questions follow: How can anyone call upon the Lord if they have not believed in Him? How shall they believe in Christ unless they hear about Him? How shall they hear without a proclaimer or witness? How can they have a witness unless one is sent? Our response must be, "Here am I; send me."

Most significantly, our Lord Jesus Christ gave specific commands to take His redemptive message to all the world. The last words of Matthew's Gospel contain what has been called the Great Commission. It would be difficult to misunderstand the words of the risen Lord to His disciples:

> Go ye therefore, and teach all nations, baptizing them in the name of the Father, and of the Son, and of the Holy Ghost: Teaching them to observe all things whatsoever I have commanded you: and, lo, I am with you alway, even unto the end of the world (Matt. 28:19-20).

Just before His ascension, Jesus said to the disciples, "Ye shall be witnesses unto me both in Jerusalem, and in all Judaea, and in Samaria, and unto the uttermost part of the earth" (Acts 1:8).

The Significance of the Missionary Enterprise

The Bible's emphasis on the missionary task is not incidental. When we obey the biblical injunction to take God's redemptive message to all the world, every aspect of our lives and our relationship to God and to one another is radically affected. In the wisdom of God, missions fills a vital place in all that we do and think as Christians.

God's True Nature and Purpose

First, missions reveals to us God's true nature and purpose. Human efforts to find God and understand Him spawned many misconceptions. The pagan religions saw God as a fearful and destructive being, always seeking to harm people on earth and as one who could be placated only by sacrifices—sometimes human—and incantations. The Greeks had numerous gods with different functions and powers, but all were to be dreaded. They resembled oversized human beings who possessed all of the sinful and lustful human habits on a larger scale. They were hateful, violent, and self-centered. The numerous Roman gods were used mainly to forward Roman political ambitions.

But our Lord Jesus Christ revealed the true nature of God as Heavenly Father, the loving and compassionate God. God's love is responsible for our salvation. "God so loved the world, that he gave his only begotten Son, that whosoever believeth in him should not perish, but have everlasting life" (John 3:16). The human mind cannot grasp the total meaning of that gift of love. The expression "so loved the world" does not define the totality of God's love, but it provides a glimpse of its quality by showing what love did. God gave His Son for our sins. The hymn "The Ninety and Nine" expresses this well:

> But none of the ransomed ever knew
> How deep were the waters crossed;
> Nor how dark was the night that the Lord
>   passed thro'
> Ere He found His sheep that was lost.

This redemptive love seems to be the only clue to the most profound question ever to face humanity: Why did God create the world and human beings when He knew beforehand that the world would reject and crucify His only Son? The reason lies in the nature of God's love: He longed for those in His own image who would freely love Him in return. This is suggested by a Scripture in Isaiah 43. The prophet reminded Israel that it had been ungrateful for God's blessings and had neglected its worship and sacrifice; despite this, God said, "I, even I, am He that blotteth out thy transgrsssions for mine own sake" (v. 25). For His own sake, because of His great love, God made us and redeemed us that He might know our love and fellowship.

God's Redemptive Love

Second, missions is God's plan to enable His children to bless all the world with the story of His redemptive love. Our Lord's concern for the world was displayed in Luke 10:25-37 when a lawyer tested Him with a question about how to find eternal life and quoted the Law, "Thou shalt love the Lord thy God with all thy heart, and with all thy soul, and with all thy strength, and with all thy mind; and thy neighbour as thyself" (v. 27). When Jesus approved this answer, the lawyer raised a question the Jewish teachers had been arguing for centuries: "Who is my neighbour?" (v. 29). Jesus then told the story of the good Samaritan who helped a man who had been robbed and beaten and who had been ignored by a priest and a Levite. Jesus inquired, "Which of these three, . . ., was neighbor to him that fell among the thieves?" The lawyer was forced to give the right answer: "He that shewed mercy on him" (v. 37).

Our world is finally beginning to grasp the meaning of our Lord's parable. Every large-scale catastrophe in any part of the world today, whether a destructive earthquake, a drought, a flood, or an atomic disaster, promptly brings a universal response to provide food, clothing, medical aid, and technological expertise. Furthermore, one of the most encouraging features of the twentieth century has been the developing recognition of the worth and dignity of all human beings as our neighbors. This spirit is beginning to penetrate worldwide organizations and even governments in their attitutdes toward others.

Christians have played a large role in this developing sense of world community, but they have a better blessing for needy people. This better gift should not be a substitute for meeting material needs, but to provide for these physical needs alone is inadequate. Our Lord said, "Life is more than meat, and the body is more than raiment" (Luke 12:23). Without lessening our response to physical human needs, we must take the unspeakable gift of Jesus Christ to all who are needy: to the down-and-out and to the up-and-out. All of them need the universal message that "if thou shalt confess with thy mouth the Lord Jesus, and shalt believe in thine heart that God hath raised him from the dead, thou shalt be saved" (Rom. 10:9). This message can transform the hearts of people, and only that can defeat racial, sexual, and cultural discriminations. In Christ "there is neither Jew nor Greek, there is neither bond nor free, there is neither male nor female: for ye are all one in Christ Jesus" (Gal. 3:28). Ultimately the only solution for all hatred, violence, crime, and war is this new heart. It provides an internal dynamic rather than the threat of external compulsion.

Christian Fulfillment

Third, missions is God's method of enabling Christians to achieve the greatest fulfillment in their own lives. A characteristic pattern of our modern industrial world has been the failure of people to find meaning in life. Building a happy home, engaging in an important occupation, and achieving financial security and intellectual growth seem no longer to challenge either young people or mature men and women. Boredom, dissatisfaction, and frustration grip our society. The number of young people turning to drugs or committing suicide because they find no meaning in life is growing at an alarming rate. How different from the fulfillment and joy that comes from the most menial tasks when a person is conscious of the fact that he is participating in the plan of God for his life.

A charming story from the Old Testament may illustrate how the most humble tasks of life become meaningful when we recognize God's hand in our lives. In 1 Chronicles 9:14-27, the historian described the work assigned to each of the Levites who dwelt in Jerusalem. Four were named as "chief porters" of the house of God (v. 26). To accomplish the duties assigned them, "they lodged round about the house of

God, because the charge was upon them, and the opening thereof every morning pertained to them" (v. 27). This task involved no boredom or frustration because God's charge was upon them.

This is the source of joy and refreshment that all Christians know: The charge of God is upon them to witness to His grace, whatever their occupation may be, and by prayers and gifts help in sending others to witness in places where they cannot go.

Actually, this is the very meaning of Christian stewardship. God is the owner of all things—our lives, our talents, our money, and our service. Even if our Lord had not commissioned us to be witnesses to the world in missions, we would still have to account to the owner of the vineyard for how we have used His gifts which were entrusted to us for a brief season. Our stewardship of life includes the central purpose of God to witness to all the world. Christ said, "As my Father hath sent me, even so send I you" (John 20:21); we have become stewards of the grace of God by this commission. In accepting this commission, we attain the highest good and greatest fulfillment in our lives.

This wonderful privilege that is ours has a solemn note. If Christians neglect to witness to the world about God's redemption in Christ, no one else will or can. One day while lecturing in his theology class, Dr. W. T. Conner, one of Southern Baptists' ablest theologians, said:

> After Christ's death on the cross, the angels of God could well have bowed before the Father and said, "Let us go tell all the world about Thy redemptive purpose and Christ's sacrifice for the sins of the world." But God could have replied, "No, you cannot take this message to the world because you are not qualified. Only those men and women who have been lost and then have experienced the saving grace of Jesus Christ are qualified to witness to that grace."

Christian Service

Finally, missions brings to Christians the privilege of a loving fellowship in Christian service. When our Lord commissioned us to go into all the world and make disciples and teach them all things, He knew the task was too large for one person or one congregation. The task demands that Christians work together in this worldwide mission. The most important single factor causing Baptists to cooperate in general organizations in America was the biblical injunction to witness to all nations.

One of the unfailing joys of Paul was his sense of comradeship with his fellow workers in the missionary task. He addressed them as true yokefellows, laborers together with God, fellow helpers, fellow laborers, work fellows, blessed brethren, and, for those whom he had won to Christ, the title beloved sons. As he wrote his fellow workers in the church at Philippi, Paul expressed this loving spirit in words both beautiful and moving. He called them "my brethren dearly beloved and longed for, my joy and my crown, . . . my dearly beloved" (Phil. 4:1). This fellowship in the stewardship of the grace of God lightened Paul's burdens and increased his courage in the face of fierce adversaries. Christians since Paul have testified that "the fellowship of kindred minds is like to that above."

Paul recognized that when Christians began working together they would observe that they differed from one another in many ways. He addressed their diversity in spiritual gifts, for example. Paul said that some Christians may have numerous and significant spiritual gifts, while others may have few and seemingly unimportant gifts; but the spiritual gifts of all Christians are important in the work of Christ. The apostle compared the body of Christ to the physical body, pointing out that every part of the physical body plays an important role in the well-being of the person. He even said that the "more feeble" (12:22) parts of the body may be more necessary than some of the more visible parts. But all Christians, he continued, can exercise that "more excellent" gift of the Spirit, which is love. In succeeding verses Paul declared that love is greater than speaking in tongues, prophecy, knowledge, faith, and total self-sacrifice. Faith, hope, and love are the great fundamentals of joyful Christian service, and the greatest of these is love (1 Cor. 12:12 to 13:13).

In a word of summary, then, the Bible is a missionary book from Genesis to Revelation. The ground of missions is the love of God as revealed in His redemptive purpose in Jesus Christ. The practice of missions brings each of us to a personal participation in God's redemptive purpose; it makes us representatives of Christ to a lost world; it fulfills life's supreme stewardship; it brings the fullest meaning to our earthly existence, and it offers the privilege of a cooperative Christian fellowship in service that enriches the journey.

Note

1. W. O. Carver, *The Course of Christian Missions* (New York: Fleming H. Revell Co., 1932), p. 22.

2
Baptists Facing the Challenge of World Missions

How have Baptists in America endeavored to organize themselves to witness for Jesus Christ to the ends of the earth? I have limited my discussion to Baptists in America, and even more narrowly to those Baptist bodies which have influenced Southern Baptists in their efforts to form missionary organizations.

Baptist Difficulties in Organizing for Missions

Baptists have always faced problems when attempting to organize for missionary and other benevolent work. There have been several reasons for this.

Congregation-Centered Polity

In the first place, Baptist polity has always been congregation centered. A conviction of Baptists has always been that no pope or prelate, no civil or ecclesiastical monarch, no oligarchy, no ascending judicature of churches or denominational bodies like those of the Presbyterians, or any other extra-church authority may usurp the right of a local congregation to exercise its autonomy and freedom.

One of the glories of Baptists on the early American frontier, and probably one of the reasons for their rapid growth in that period, was the fact that when a person felt a call to preach the gospel, he did not need seek the approval of some distant ecclesiastical organization. His local congregation could license him to give expression to the fire in his bones.

This grass-roots polity allowed the prospective preacher's immediate peers to determine his qualifications "to exercise his gifts in public."

These farmer-preachers roamed the American frontier with a simple philosophy: My Lord has not sent me to tell a few people a great many things but to tell many people a few things. These preachers knew these few things well from experience and studying the Scriptures. They went everywhere establishing churches, observing the ordinances, burying the dead, and performing marriages. This kind of congregational autonomy was practiced for many years before the development of any kind of extra-church organizations, and it gave American Baptists a strong sense of the primacy and adequacy of the local congregation in all church matters.

Passion for Individual and Institutional Freedom

In the second place, Baptists have found organizing for cooperative work difficult because of their intense passion for both individual and institutional freedom. Their historical background in England and America reinforced their adherence to the biblical doctrines of liberty of conscience and freedom from civil or ecclesiastical coercion. In America they felt the heavy hand of persecution in practically all of the early colonies. In Virginia, in particular, their sufferings took a long time to heal. Actually, all religious discrimination against Baptists did not end until 1833, almost two centuries after the first Baptist church was established in America. This passion for freedom, combined with the nature of their local church polity, was probably the principal reason American Baptists did not organize their first association until 1707, about sixty-eight years after the founding of their first church. Their second association was not formed for another forty-four years and only then through the work of a former member of the first association who had moved to a distant colony and found it too far to journey for associational meetings.

Baptist Diversity

A third difficulty faced by Baptists in their efforts to organize for missions was the inherent diversity in Baptist ranks. It is true, of course, that individual diversity is a common characteristic of all humanity. Criminologists report that no two persons have identical fingerprints, footprints, lip prints, or hair structures. Anthropologists have not discovered two tribes having identical cultural patterns. Psychologists assert that no two humans have identical mind-sets because each person has unique genetic and environmental factors. We should not be surprised, then, that Baptists, reared with different genetic and environmental backgrounds and insistent upon the right of individual interpretations of the Scriptures and complete liberty of expression without coercion, have formed dozens of separate denominational bodies and have developed numerous parties within their denominations.

Most of us can identify with this situation. When I surrendered to preach in 1936, I was totally shocked to discover this diversity in doctrines and polity among my fellow Southern Baptist preachers. I had been engaged in investigative work for our government, and my few contacts with theological differences among Baptists had not prepared me for the diversity in doctrine and polity that I found in Baptist life when I resigned my governmental post and returned to school to prepare for the ministry.

I entered Baylor University in 1936 to sit at the feet of J. B. Tidwell. At that time he was president of the Baptist General Convention of Texas, head of the Bible Department at Baylor, and sought constantly to express Baptist orthodoxy. In my first year at the university, he taught a class called Christian Teachings, in which I enrolled. So far as I know, all of us in the class, both teacher and pupils, thoroughly believed in the total inspiration of the Bible: that it was written "by men divinely inspired, and is a perfect treasure of heavenly instruction; that it has God for its author, salvation for its end, and truth, without any mixture of error, as its matter." You will recognize this definition as being taken from the 1963 Kansas City confession of faith adopted by the Southern Baptist Convention. This was the same language used in the Memphis Articles adopted by the Southern Baptist Convention in 1925, which copied an article from the New Hampshire Confession of Faith of 1833. Evidently, the New Hampshire wording came from the writings of John Locke, the seventeenth-century English philosopher.

One day in this class on Christian Teachings Dr. Tidwell startled all of us by stating that he believed that the crucifixion of Christ took place on Wednesday of Passover Week, not on Friday as most of us had been taught. He said that he based this belief on his interpretation of the "high" day of the feast which was on Wednesday. A spirited discussion followed and continued in the dormitory and cafeteria.

Dr. Tidwell exploded another bombshell a few days later when he said:

> Most of you, I presume, are premillennialists who believe that all Christians will reign for a thousand years on the earth after the return of our Lord. But if you will carefully exegete Revelation 20:1-5, you will find that the original text says that only the *souls of martyrs* shall reign for this indefinite period. Thus, the millennium will not include all Christians and will not take place on earth but in heaven where the souls of the martyrs are.

Much more discussion ensued, of course. As far as I know, few of the students of that class were in full agreement with their distinguished teacher on these things. I found also that the students differed with the teacher and with each other on many details of their doctrinal views on baptism, the Lord's Supper, church discipline, church and state, dispensationalism, theological education, and other teachings of the Scriptures. This kind of diversity in interpreting the Scriptures has been a hindrance as our Baptist people have endeavored to form organizations for missions and other benevolent work.

Ongoing Difficulties

Finally, it has been difficult for Baptists to organize bodies to cooperate together because they have learned from experience that their disagreements and controversies can never be finally settled. Baptist polity does not permit one congregation to force another congregation to accept its scriptural interpretations. No individual or organized body has the authority to pronounce a particular interpretation of the Scriptures as infallible and require all Baptists to conform. Baptists have no infallible pope or institution for this purpose. Consequently, old controversies never die. They constantly arise in the same pattern or modified in form. Baptists need to have a great deal of patience with one another in their diversity.

Despite these difficulties, Baptists have recognized their obligation to take the gospel message to the uttermost parts of the earth. They have also understood this task required some kind of organization through which they could work together in obedience to the Lord's command. During almost three and one-half centuries since the first Baptist church in America was formed in 1639, Baptists have attempted to meet the missionary challenge in a variety of ways.

Missions by Individuals and Churches (1639-1755)

The first evangelistic and missionary activity by Baptists in America developed from the initiative of individuals, often with the cooperation of the little congregations which they were serving. They ranged near and far, sometimes taking brief missionary tours over a large area of the wilderness. At night they were welcomed into the homes of those to whom they preached, and their principal expenses were the horses they used for the journeys. Large volumes have been written to describe the work of these men, so it will not be practicable to attempt that here. Typical of them were John Clarke of

Providence Plantations; John Myles, the stalwart Welsh preacher in Massachusetts; William Screven of Maine and later of South Carolina; Paul Palmer of North Carolina; and William Sojourner of Virginia, who later migrated to North Carolina. This was the only type of Baptist missionary work done in America during the long period from 1639 to 1755, more than a century.

In 1707 Baptists formed their first association at Philadelphia. The pattern for this kind of extra-church organization came from England, where it had emerged among Baptists in the army of Oliver Cromwell during the civil wars of the 1640s and 1650s. As in England, the first associations were formed only for fellowship and mutual counsel.

The Philadelphia Baptist Association was composed of messengers sent by affiliating churches, usually the pastors of the churches. It met in a very informal fashion, disdaining the choice of a regular moderator or preparing a program in advance. It claimed no authority over the churches affiliated with it. Despite this, however, many Baptist leaders and their churches opposed the formation of any kind of extra-church body for any purpose. Partly because of this resistance and for other reasons, the Philadelphia Association published an essay "on the power and duty of an association of churches" in 1749. An effort was made to define "what power an Association of churches hath, and what duty is incumbent on an Association; and prevent the contempt with which some are ready to treat such an assembly, and also to prevent any future generations from claiming more power than they ought—lording over the churches."

Despite the assertion in the essay of the Philadelphia Association that "each particular church hath a complete power and authority from Jesus Christ," many Baptists in America still had a great deal of "contempt" for the associational structure. A second association was formed in America in 1751 by a former member of the Philadelphia Association who had moved to South Carolina. After the formation of the Charleston Association in 1751 by Oliver Hart, the number of associations in America increased slowly during the remainder of the century.

Missions Through Baptist Associations (1755-1800)

In 1755 the Philadelphia Association voted to appoint two missionaries to work in North Carolina. This action was probably influenced by the appeal of Benjamin Miller, pastor of the Scotch Plains Baptist Church in New Jersey, who at that time was engaged in an effort to form a church at what was known as the Jersey Settlement on the Yadkin River of North Carolina. Miller was one of the two missionaries appointed, and he continued his work at the Jersey Settlement. At about the same time Oliver Hart, pastor of the Charleston church in South Carolina and a leader in the work of the Charleston Association, visited Philadelphia to find a missionary for appointment by the Charleston Association to the same Jersey Settlement of North Carolina. John Gano, who had already worked on that field with Benjamin Miller, was named by the Charleston Association to work at the Jersey Settlement mission. It was formed into a church and joined the Charleston Association in 1759.

This action by the Philadelphia and Charleston associations marked the beginning of a missionary program through the associations. As new associations began to form in both the North and the South during the last half of the eighteenth century, they also adopted mission work as a part of their denominational program. A good example of the manner in which associations handled their missionary work may be seen in the minutes of the Shaftsbury Association of Vermont. The association outlined its plan in the minutes of its meeting on June 2-3, 1802. Its objective was:

> To enable the Association to send able and faithful ministers to preach the gospel, and endeavor to build up the visible cause of the Redeemer in such parts of the United States, or

the Canadas, as are destitute of gospel privileges; and, as far as they can have access, among the natives of the wilderness.

To carry out this objective, the association named a committee each year composed of twelve brethren, six of whom were to be ministers, who would take charge of the contributions from the churches, faithfully examine all candidates, determine the time and field of the appointee, and without fee or salary supervise the work being done by the several missionaries. The churches of the association made contributions to this program on a voluntary basis.

This change in the nature of the association from an informal body for fellowship and counsel into a vehicle supervising missionary work substantially increased the opposition of many Baptists to the associations. Some incidents seemed to justify Baptists' fear of the increasing power of extra-church bodies. In England, for example, a seventeenth-century general body of the General Baptists had openly violated the autonomy and freedom of the congregations affiliating with it on the grounds of preserving unity and orthodoxy. In America in 1752, the Philadelphia Association had sent a committee of its ministers to the church at Opekon, Virginia, which had appealed for help. The committee had dissolved the General Baptist congregation and formed a Particular Baptist church in its place, admitting only those former members who could prove their Particular Baptist orthodoxy. Also, in 1771, Shubal Stearns, organizer of the Sandy Creek Association of North Carolina and one of the founders of the Separate Baptist movement, had become so high-handed in dealing with the churches affiliating with the association that the association split to form three associations. Morgan Edwards, the Baptist historian, said that Stearns had evidently brought this unbaptistic use of authority from his background in Congregationalism.

The Adoption of the Society Method for Missions (1800-1845)

With all of the dissatisfaction over the increasing power of the associations, the stage was set for a change. It came through a dramatic event that took place among English Baptists. William Carey was born on August 17, 1761, to poor parents. He was apprenticed as a lad to a shoemaker. He and his family were members of the state church; but one day in a Dissenters' meeting, he heard the earnest minister expound on the text, "Let us go forth therefore unto him without the camp, bearing his reproach" (Heb. 13:13). He felt that God was talking to him, so he left the state church and joined the despised Baptists. In 1784, following a call to preach the gospel, Carey became pastor of a little Baptist church not far from his home. At his cobbler's bench during the day, he studied his Bible carefully and became convinced that Christ's commission to take the gospel into all the world was obligatory.

Carey was fired by the stories of people in faraway lands which were told him by his Uncle Peter. He pored over the little book by Captain James Cook, describing his explorations in the mysterious South sea islands. He pinned a map of the world above his cobbler's bench; as he worked, he visualized the needs of all people for the gospel. Most of all, he pondered the plain words of Paul, "How shall they hear without a preacher? And how shall they preach, except they be sent" (Rom. 10:14-15). Other Dissenters, like the Wesleys and the General Baptists, were trumpeting a gospel of free grace across England. For several reasons, even the Particular Baptists, of whom Carey was a part, were moving away from extreme predestinarianism.

Perhaps the first gleams of the modern mission movement appeared when, as a messenger from his church at Leicester to the Northampton Association, Carey was asked by the moderator, John Ryland, Sr., to propose a subject for discussion at the meeting. After a moment of hesitation, Carey boldly asked, "whether the command given to the apostles to teach all nations was not obligatory on all ministers to the end of the world." Moderator Ryland, a member of the old school, bellowed, "Sit down, young man, when God wants to convert the world He can do it without your help."

In May 1792 Carey preached a missionary message at the associational meeting from the text in Isaiah 54:2-3, which he interpreted in two propositions: "Expect great things from God; attempt great things for God." On October 2 of that year, Carey and eleven others met at Kettering and formed a society for promoting the evangelization of the world. The initial subscription for this task was thirteen pounds, ten shillings, and sixpence. Not a very propitious beginning for a movement that would shake the world to its foundations!

The missions movement in England affected Baptists in America in three important visible ways.

A New Advance in Missions

Carey's modern mission movement sparked a new advance in missionary efforts among Baptists in America. In a rather curious fashion, the new advance ricocheted off the activity of the Congregationalists, who had also been inspired by Carey's movement. In August 1812, Adoniram Judson and his wife Ann Hasseltine, who had sailed to India as missionaries for the Congregationalists, became Baptists after a lengthy study of the Scriptures and other books. They were baptized by William Ward, one of the missionaries in Carey's band in Calcutta. In November of the same year, Luther Rice, the third member of the Judson party, was also baptized by William Ward after Rice's careful study led him to the Baptist position. Both Judson and Rice wrote to Boston Baptist leaders, describing their change in convictions and asking support in their missionary efforts.

At first Baptist leaders in America hesitated to assume the support of these missionaries since they had no general denominational body of any kind. Carey wrote to Thomas Baldwin of Boston, "Do stir in this business; this is a providence which gives a new turn to American Christians to Oriental Missions." Despite England's being at war with the United States, Carey insisted that the English missionaries would not desert these new missionaries, even if American Baptists could not agree to support them.

God had been preparing Baptists in America for this experience. For a number of years Baptist leaders in Boston, Philadelphia, and Charleston had been in correspondence with the English society and their missionaries in India and had shared this missionary information with their people. In addition, a curious incident in the opening years of the nineteenth century, which appeared at first to be a harsh blow to the English missionary enterprise, actually turned out to be a blessing.

The blow was the announcement by the British East India Company that they would no longer allow English missionaries to board their boats for India. This made it necessary for English Baptist missionaries to take ship to the United States enroute to India over another line. Sometimes these dedicated missionaries of the Baptist Missionary Society of London were forced to wait for weeks in the United States before a vessel sailed from American ports to India. During that time, they were entertained in the homes of Baptists, who learned to know and love them long before Baptists in America sent out any missionaries.

Furthermore, Baptist leaders in America knew that their people were willing to support foreign mission work. Between the years 1806 and 1814, Baptists in America gave over $20,000 for foreign missions. As a matter of fact, they had provided more than $3,000 to help send the Judsons and Rice to India under the appointment of the Congregational Board.

When Baptists in America learned that the Judsons and Rice had become Baptists, they promptly organized local foreign mission societies in many of the states. More significantly, on May 18, 1814, thirty-three influential representatives from Baptist churches met at Philadelphia and organized the first Baptist general body in American history—a foreign mission society. Between 1814 and 1845, Baptists from all sections of the United States cooperated in the support of this foreign mission society, as well as two other societies: one for tract publication organized in 1824 and one for home missions formed in 1832.

Antimission and Antieffort Reaction

The formation of national missionary bodies that followed the modern mission movement by Carey aroused a strong antimission and antieffort reaction. From the 1820s to the 1840s this antieffort reaction severely impeded the cause of missions and other benevolent work in America. Leaders like John Taylor of Kentucky, Joshua Lawrence of North Carolina, Gilbert Beebe of New York, and Daniel Parker of Tennessee and Texas took up the cudgel against Baptist missions.

The reasons for this opposition were numerous. Many antimissioners claimed a theological basis for their resistance. Taking up the predestinarian theme of Augustine, Calvin, and the early Particular Baptists in England, antieffort people asserted that it was blasphemy for human beings to try to win people to Christ, to teach young men how to preach, to operate Sunday schools, or to use any other kind of human effort to forward the kingdom of God. They argued that God had already elected which individuals would be saved and which would not and that it was blasphemous to try to change what God had already arranged. These zealous defenders of God's will did not consider that a part of His elective grace was the use of human instruments to carry out His purpose. They gave little attention to the specific commissions of our Lord to go to the ends of the earth to make disciples.

Baptists in America had many other reasons for opposition to missions. The organization of extra-church bodies offended some. The intense sectionalism of the period aroused suspicion against anybody from one of the other sections. The prejudice involved in class distinctions is often found in the literature; derogatory expressions about "book-educated preachers" abound. Clerical rivalry, personal jealousy, and the constant call for money alienated many. The varieties of antimission thinking ranged from that of a man like Beebe, who opposed all human efforts in behalf of the kingdom to that of Parker, who distrusted the sincerity of the money gatherers and the extra-church organizations.

A New Organizational Option

Carey's movement provided a new organizational option for doing mission work. Many Baptists resisted the development of associations because they feared that these extra-church bodies would become too powerful and would attempt to "lord it over God's heritage." This opposition increased substantially when the associations branched out in their activities to take up mission work. Most Baptists wanted to support mission work but feared the increasing power of the associations.

The significance of the organizational pattern of William Carey did not escape their notice. He turned away from the churches and the associations for the support of his mission program. Instead, he and the mission-minded band who met in the Widow Wallis's little back parlor in Kettering in 1792 to organize the Particular Baptist Society for Foreign Missions decided to bypass the denominational bodies and form an independent *society* for missions. The missionary society idea was not a new one, for it had been used on the Continent. But it was a captivating idea for Baptists in America who were uneasy about doing mission work through associations. A. L. Vail, a Northern Baptist mission historian at the turn of this century, expressed it well:

> The churches were exceedingly jealous for their authority. We have seen how long the Philadelphia Association fumbled over

this point, and when the Warren [Association] came into being it was under keen suspicion, so that at first some of the best pastors stood aloof. This state of mind prevailed more or less everywhere, and although necessity had pushed the Associations into mission work, it had been done gingerly and from hand to mouth in the main. In this situation the society opened the way out of some of the perplexity. The Associations were based in the churches, having some organic or semi-organic relation with them, therefore they were specially and inevitably watched with reference to centralization. But start a society without any direct connection with the churches, and thus free from the suspicion of usurpation in that measure of authority essential to effectiveness, and there would be plainer sailing. Mission-minded brethren might tolerate in the society what they would not in the Association, and omission-minded brethren would keep out of the way by keeping out of the society. This might have constituted to judicious and irenic leaders a reason for the society, and probably it was the chief reason with those who thought thoroughly.[1]

For the reasons given by Dr. Vail, Baptists in America immediately and almost unanimously began to withdraw from associational mission programs and to form separate and independent societies for missions. By 1810 most of the associations had discontinued mission activity, and mission societies sprang up in all parts of the United States. The first Baptist general body formed in 1814 was patterned after the Carey society plan, basing its membership on financial gifts and claiming complete independence from Baptist churches and associations. This was also true of the second Baptist general body organized at Washington, D. C. in 1824 for the publication of tracts, as well as the American Baptist Home Mission Society organized in 1832 in New York City.

The significant nature of this development has not generally been recognized by Baptist historians. By withdrawing from a program of missions conducted by associations, Baptists sought to ensure that the associations could not infringe upon the freedom and autonomy of the local churches. Baptists were deliberately choosing an antidenominational method of doing mission work to safeguard their churches from having "overlords." They preferred to safeguard church independency by rejecting denominational cooperation. The missionary and tract societies formed between 1814 and 1832 were strictly antidenominational. Each society was completely independent of the others. The denomination was divided into benevolent slices. The societies had a financial rather than a denominational base, and they promoted rivalry for funds without reference to the welfare of the entire denomination.

This deliberate antidenominational stance was reflected in the 1820s when Richard Furman and others tried to unify the societies into a denominational-type body, but their efforts were decisively rebuffed. The antidenominational character of the societies was also illustrated in the 1840s during the abolitionist-slavery controversy. One of the members in the Home Mission Society suggested that the society poll the Baptist churches in the United States in an effort to determine their desires in the controversy. Promptly, Dr. Francis Wayland, at that time president of Brown University and the leading Baptist of the North, rose to a point of order to say, "Churches are not related in any way to this society and should not be polled." He went on to point out that missionary societies could never be representative denominational bodies because of the nature of their structure.

Thus, before 1845 Baptists in America had chosen the antidenominational society pattern for carrying on their mission and other benevolent work, and they had deliberately separated their missionary organizations from the churches and associations in an effort to safeguard the freedom and autonomy of their churches.

The Southern Baptist Mission Structure (1845-1900)

The principal architect of the new Southern Baptist Convention was William B. Johnson of South Carolina. He was the only person at the consultative convention in Augusta,

Georgia, in 1845 who had been present at the organization of the first general body of Baptists in 1814. He had served in 1814 as a member of the committee to prepare the constitution for that foreign mission society and had later served as its president. Johnson was an astute, experienced, and dedicated Baptist whose writings revealed outstanding insights and abilities. He had been reared in South Carolina under the influence of Richard Furman, whose entire ministry had emphasized the necessity of denominational unity and cooperation.

Johnson was president of the South Carolina Baptist Convention in 1845. He called a special session of that body to meet just one week before the consultative meeting of all Southern Baptists was convened at Augusta. The principal purpose of the special session of the South Carolina body seems to have been to hear a long and scholarly address by Johnson about the issues which would be faced at the coming consultative meeting. Johnson said that he had reluctantly come to the conclusion that there must be separation from the older missionary societies which had refused to appoint southern missionaries. He compared the situation to that in which Paul and Barnabas had sharp contention and separated one from the other on the second missionary journey. The parting of Paul and Barnabas had turned out for good because as a result "two lines of service were opened for the benefit of the churches." He continued:

> Such, I trust, will be the result of the separation between the Baptists of these United States in their general benevolent institutions. When we embarked in the cause of Foreign Missions, the union of the whole denomination was necessary, for it was then comparatively small. But now, such is the state of things, that we may part asunder and open two lines of service to the heathen and the destitute, instead of one only, and the vast increase in our numbers, and the wide extent of territory, over which we are spread, seem to indicate the hope, that our separation will be attended with no sharpness of contention,

with no bitterness of spirit. We are all the servants of the same Master, "desirous of doing the will of God from the heart." Let us, then, in generous rivalry, "provoke each other to love and good works."

Johnson then noted that Baptists had been functioning for years through the use of separate and independent societies for foreign missions, home missions, and publication of tracts. He urged that a new pattern be adopted by Southern Baptists. He proposed the formation of "one Convention, embodying the whole Denomination, together with separate and distinct Boards, for each object of benevolent enterprise, located at different places, and all amenable to the Convention."[2]

The intent of Johnson's grand design was to heal the historical breach between the denomination and the missionary enterprise. Through what he called a "judicious concentration," his goals may be summed up as follows. First, he desired to eliminate the prevailing disunity which came from paring the denomination into benevolent slices. Second, he wanted to develop a strong denominational consciousness which would elicit, combine, and direct the energies of the whole denomination in one sacred effort for the propagation of the gospel. He believed that kind of denominational consciousness required Southern Baptists to develop a denominational body which would promote not only home and foreign missions but also other activities like Christian education, a publications, and Sunday school training. These adjuncts would undergird and support the missionary enterprise. Third, he aimed to make all of the benevolent agencies amenable to the convention itself, thus providing a representative and responsive denominational body.

When the consultative convention of Southern Baptists met the following week at Augusta, Georgia, Johnson's proposals were adopted in large measure. Article V of the new constitution provided that the Convention would elect at each triennial meeting as many Boards of Managers as in its judgment were necessary for carrying out the benevolent objects the Convention chose to promote. At this time the Convention decided to promote only two benevolences: home and foreign missions.

Unfortunately, the Convention also adopted in Articles III and XI of their new constitution the same method of financing the work of the Convention as the one used by the older societies. This also determined the basis of representation at the Convention and made designated giving to the agencies (instead of to the Convention itself) the method of financial support.

Thus, the structure adopted in 1845 was hybrid in nature: a unifying denominational body in Article V of the constitution and an antidenominational body in Articles III and XI. The result was the development of tensions between the denominational and antidenominational elements for the remainder of the century. These tensions expressed themselves in several forms.

Visible Marring of Denominational Thrust

During the next half century, there was a visible marring of the denominational thrust of the Convention. Many Southern Baptist leaders wanted to follow the grand design of Johnson by organizing additional boards to promote publication, Sunday School work, and ministerial education. However, at the 1845 meeting only two boards were formed: one for foreign and one for home missions. When the Convention itself did not agree to form boards for other benevolences, Southern Baptist leaders organized society-type structures outside of the Convention: one for publication work in 1847, one for Sunday school promotion in 1857, and one for education of the ministry in 1859. Later on, women's work (1888), youth work (1895), and men's work (1907) were developed outside of the Convention's structure.

Making Structural Changes

The tension in the structure of the Convention brought constant efforts to make changes. The financial basis of representation and the use of designated giving caused the Convention to be neither representative nor responsive. As one reads through the minutes of the regular meetings of the Convention, one is struck by the number of calls for change. Some wanted the financial basis changed to associational representation, some preferred state convention representation, and some a numerical type of representation. Many of the complaints urged a church basis of representation, particularly after the outbreak of the Landmark controversy. Under the financial pattern, the number of representatives from churches was often small. In 1901, for example, an editorial in the *Word and Way*, the Missouri Baptist paper, asserted that not a single representative from a Baptist church was accredited to the last Convention meeting because the financial amount was too great. The editor felt that the important place of the local churches was being threatened by this situation.

Accepting Designated Gifts

The making of designated gifts to the agencies resulted in a penniless Convention. Perhaps this was not a major problem since the expenses of most of the officers of the Convention were provided by their societies, churches, associations, or whatever body they represented. This was an impossible situation, however, when legitimate Convention expenses began to develop. For example, the printing of the annual minutes of the Convention required the use of designated mission funds. The Convention treasurers had nothing to do since all of the funds were handled by the treasurers of the boards to which the funds were designated. In fact, the treasurer of the Convention made no regular reports to the Convention for many decades after the Convention was formed.

Raising Mission Funds

The methodology used for raising mission funds brought constant problems. The old society pattern required that agents be employed to visit churches, associations, and meetings of the state bodies to appeal for funds for their particular benevolence. This was an expensive method since the agents' expenses and salaries had to be paid out of the offerings they secured. In 1875, for example, the Home Mission Board collected $19,359.81 during the entire year, and 44 percent of this was needed for the agents' expenses and salaries. The percentage was higher in many years.

This was also a haphazard method. Many things could affect the amount of the offering an agent was able to secure. He might not be able to get to the church because of rain or an epidemic; a recent visit by an agent of another benevolence might garner all the offering a church could give. The stability of the agency for whom the agent was collecting funds was in constant peril because of such haphazard collections. Before the adoption of the Cooperative Program, the mission boards were forced to borrow large sums of money from banks in order to keep their agencies functioning until offerings were received. It was impossible to estimate how successful the efforts to raise funds might be, so the mission programs were operated on a hope-so basis.

Unscriptural

This method was unscriptural. Money raising was separated from spirituality and scriptural injunctions. In Texas, for example, as in many other states, mission offerings were successful only about two times each year: just before the Southern Baptist Convention met in the spring and just before the state convention gatherings in the fall. In the cowboy terminology of west Texas, there were two roundups each year: the fall roundup and the spring roundup. These special drives for mission offerings usually brought a great deal of preaching about missions, but training in scriptural stewardship and the demands of the Great Commission was minimal during the remainder of the year in many churches. The splendid educational program of Woman's Missionary Union, later supplemented by the Layman's Missionary movement, helped to begin to correct this difficiency.

By the turn of the century, Southern Baptist leaders recognized that the society pattern of designated giving and the financial basis of representation were simply not adequate for the challenge of the new century. Voices across the territory of the Southern Baptist Convention called for an improved convention structure for carrying out Christ's Commission.

Notes

1. Albert L. Vail, *The Morning Hour of American Baptist Missions* (Philadelphia: American Baptist Publication Society, 1907), pp. 150-51.
2. See the *Edgefield Advertiser* (Edgefield, S. C.) 7 May 1845, which contained a copy of Dr. Johnson's message.

―――――――――――― 3 ――――――――――――

The Cooperative Program and World Missions

Southern Baptists made excellent progress in statistical growth between 1845 and about 1900, despite their unsatisfactory organizational structure. They were very conscious of the obligation of the Great Commission, and their zeal overcame the weaknesses of their denominational structure. Their constituency increased from 351,951 in 1845 to 1,657,996 in 1900—a rate of growth faster than that of the population during the same period. For many reasons, the first years of Convention life showed small mission gifts, amounting in 1846 to but $11,735.22 for foreign missions and $1,824.00 for home or domestic missions. These figures, taken from the Convention reports, may not give the true picture of mission gifts. Perhaps this is the reason the *Encyclopedia of Southern Baptists* does not begin listing mission gifts of the Convention until 1885, when the total was $202,170. By 1900 mission gifts increased to $881,219. The large increase in membership and mission gifts probably can be attributed more to the widespread spirit of evangelism and missions in the local churches than to the effectiveness of the denominational structure. This is suggested by the fact that the number of local congregations affiliating with the Convention increased from 4,126 in 1845 to 19,558 in 1900, reporting baptisms of 23,222 in 1845 and 80,465 in 1900.

Southern Baptist Advance

Statistics alone reveal the spectacular advance of Southern Baptists and their Convention, beginning about 1900. Southern Baptists leaped from their place as one of the average-size denominations in 1900 to become the largest non-Roman Catholic denomination in the United States in 1985. From their 1,657,996 membership in 1900 in the South alone, their numbers increased to 14,486,403 in 1985 in all fifty states. Sunday school enrollment increased from 670,569 in 1900 to 7,960,796 in 1985. Mission gifts leaped from $881,219 in 1900 to $610,668,080 in 1985. In 1900, the Convention operated three boards (Foreign Mission Board, Home Mission Board, and Sunday School Board) and several loosely related auxiliaries (The Southern Baptist Theological Seminary, Woman's Missionary Union, and Baptist Young People's Union) in a structure that was not representative or responsive and was inadequate for effective and efficient ministry because of its financial methodology.

In a remarkable advance after about 1900, the Convention did much more than surge forward statistically. By 1985 it was operating four boards (Foreign Mission Board, Home Mission Board, Sunday School Board, and the Annuity Board), eight institutions (six seminaries, the Seminary External Education Division, and the Southern Baptist Foundation), seven commissions (for Black ministerial education, men's work, Christian life, education, history, radio and television, and stewardship), and two important standing committees (on the denominational calendar and on public affairs). The Convention maintained close ties with Woman's Missionary Union, the Baptist World Alliance, and the American Bible Society.

All of these functions were correlated and strengthened by a representative Executive Committee. Furthermore, the Convention had moved dramatically to develop a new financial structure and methodology called the Cooperative Program, which was evaluated by the Executive Committee of the

Convention in the dark days of the financial depression of the 1930s as "the greatest step forward in Kingdom finance Southern Baptists have ever taken."

What have been the reasons for this significant forward leap after about 1900 in Southern Baptist life? Some causes behind the rapid advance are complex and interacting, but one of the most important factors in the twentieth century has been the radically improved organizational structure of the Convention. The hybrid structure of the nineteenth century simply could not have supported the kind of growth Southern Baptists have had in this century.

Historians will doubtless point to three important factors involving the structure of the Southern Baptist Convention that undergirded this remarkable thrust of the twentieth century.

A New Sense of Identity

In the closing decades of the nineteenth century, Southern Baptists developed a new denominational consciousness or sense of identity. When Southern Baptists formed their Convention in 1845, the lack of denominational consciousness prevented them from taking the large step away from the old society pattern of mobilizing for missions and replacing it with a pattern which emphasized denominational unity.

This lack of a denominational consciousness surfaced in the consultative meeting of 1845. The formation of boards other than the two for foreign and domestic missions was rejected. An editorial by the editor of the *Christian Index* of Georgia, written after the close of the consultative convention in 1845, urged the formation of a board for publication work. John L. Waller, editor of the *Western Baptist Review* of Kentucky protested vigorously, saying, "We solemnly enter our protest against withdrawing from the Bible and Publication societies, merely because their Boards are located north of Mason and Dixon's line."

Beginning with the Civil War, however, a sense of Southern

Baptist denominational solidarity began to deepen. The intense sectionalism that brought the military conflict, the cohesive nature of the war, the extension of the bitterness of the conflict by the Reconstruction experience until 1877, and the common pattern of suffering among the Southern people combined to draw Southern Baptists into a closer relationship with their own organization and institutions.

Furthermore, the denominational nature of the new Southern Baptist Convention structure, as seen in Article V, encouraged a single denominational loyalty. Baptists began to recognize that the unified nature of the Convention promoted an interboard cooperation that had not been developed in the independent society plan. For example, when Basil Manly, Jr., was pleading for the formation of the first Sunday School Board in 1863, he emphasized the fact that good literature prepared for one part of the Convention's work could be duplicated for other sections and would constitute a valuable tool for providing literature of a uniformly high quality.

Two significant events probably accelerated the development of a strong denominational consciousness by Southern Baptists. One was the attempt by the Home Mission Society of New York to undermine the work of the Home Mission Board of the South by flooding the Southern states with Northern missionaries after 1865. This heated controversy continued for over two decades. It served to educate Southern Baptists in the need of being loyal to their denominational body.

The work of the Home Mission Board was so damaged that in 1882 the Convention moved the board's headquarters from Marion, Alabama, to Atlanta, Georgia, and replaced the corresponding secretary. The new executive was I. T. Tichenor, an eloquent, denominationally minded genius, who did much to develop this sense of denominational identity among Southern Baptists. He probably laid the foundation for the Cooperative Program by his vision of systematic giving. The comity agreements with northern societies that grew out of his secretaryship brought much visibility to the denominational advance of Southern Baptists.

The other event that played a significant role in the southern sense of identity was the controversy of the 1890s between the Northern publication society and the second Sunday School Board, organized in 1891. This controversy over who should supply the South with Sunday School literature was called by Dr. Tichenor "the greatest denominational struggle of the period." The turning point in the controversy occurred at the meeting of the Southern Baptist Convention in 1897 when the work of the Southern board was attacked from the platform of the Convention. The dramatic defense of Southern denominationalism by W. E. Hatcher revealed the extent to which the denominational consciousness of Southern leaders had developed.

Thus, by about 1900, Southern Baptists were reflecting a new and aggressive denominational consciousness which would provide a strong base for advance with the opening of the new century.

A New Concept of Organizational Autonomy

A second factor that led to the remarkable advance of Southern Baptists in the twentieth century was the development of a new concept of organizational autonomy. Many Baptists had objected to the formation of extra-church bodies like the association and state conventions. This attitude lingered among some Southern Baptists, who viewed with alarm the increasing activities of the Southern Baptist Convention. One reason for the instant popularity of the Landmark movement of J. R. Graves was his emphasis on local church autonomy. Graves himself attacked the Convention and its Foreign Mission Board in 1859 on the grounds that they were endangering the autonomy of the authoritative New Testament churches affiliating with them.

The disciples of Graves continued to attack the Convention on these grounds. T. P. Crawford, a missionary of the Convention in China, wrote a vitriolic tract in 1892 called "Churches to the Front," in which he blasted the Convention for assuming authority that belonged only to the churches.

Another Landmark disciple, S. A. Hayden of Texas, mounted a vendetta during the 1890s against the work of the mission board of the Baptist General Convention of Texas. After much disruption of the work of Texas Baptists, the Texas convention voted in 1897 to refuse Hayden a seat at the annual meeting. Hayden promptly responded with the Landmark argument that all general bodies are made up of churches who delegate their New Testament authority to the extra-church body, so whoever is elected by a church must be seated by the general body. In the ensuing discussion, Moderator R. C. Buckner of the Texas convention ruled that conventions are not composed of churches, but that all extra-church bodies like associations, state conventions, and the Southern Baptist Convention are made up of *messengers* who bring no authority from the churches and carry none back to the churches from the general bodies.

This emerging concept concerning the nature of general bodies played an important part in the thinking of Southern Baptists. It asserted that general bodies received their authority from the consensus of representatives from churches, not from the churches themselves. Under this concept the formation of denominational bodies for missionary and other benevolent work could never threaten the autonomy of the churches or any other Baptist body.

This concept probably led to the change in the opening words of the constitution of the Southern Baptist Convention in 1907, when the Hayden-Bogard controversy was at its height. Prior to that time the constitution referred to the *delegates* making up the Convention, but in 1907 the word *messengers* was substituted. This nomenclature emphasized the nonauthoritative nature of those sent by their churches. Under succeeding revisions of the constitution, the word *messenger* became the sole nomenclature. Today the Convention's constitution states that it exercises no authority over any other Baptist body and that the Convention is autonomous in its own sphere. This concept of authority by messenger consensus has eliminated the fear that the Southern Baptist Convention may attempt to exercise authority over other Baptist bodies.

Elimination of Antidenominational Patterns

The third structural contribution to the unusual forward thrust of the Convention in this century has been the elimination of the antidenominational patterns inherited from the older societies. In a single generation after the opening of the twentieth century, the Southern Baptist Convention totally revised its structure to eliminate the antidenominational patterns of the society method. These structural weaknesses were replaced by the formation of the Executive Committee in 1917, the development of the Cooperative Program in 1925, and the adoption of a new basis of representation in 1931.

One of the most important of these revisions was the adoption of the Cooperative Program in 1925. It dealt with the most visible weakness of the old society pattern, namely the unsatisfactory financial methodology involved in designated giving. The Cooperative Program has contributed to the advance of Southern Baptists in this century.

The Development of the Cooperative Program

The Cooperative Program of 1925 was the fulfillment of much prayer, study, and planning over a period of more than two decades and involving scores of people. At the turn of the century, Southern Baptist leaders were calling for a better structure to support the missionary enterprise. Georgia Baptists, for example, presented resolutions to the Southern Baptist Convention in 1898, urging it to make a special effort to "better organize and equip themselves for the mighty work which lies before them in the century to come." As a result the Convention appointed a Committee on Cooperation in 1899 for this study. During the Layman's Missionary movement in 1907, there were calls for "more religion in business," but many voices echoed J. B. Gambrell's pithy response, "We need more business in religion."

In 1913 John E. White of Georgia introduced a resolution calling for the appointment of seven judicious men, headed by the Convention's president, to form a commission which would

> make a careful study and a thorough examination of the organization, plans and methods of this body, with a view to determine whether or not they are best adapted for eliciting, combining and directing the energies of Southern Baptists and for securing the highest efficiency of our forces and the fullest possible enlistment of our people for the work of the Kingdom.

Thereafter an Efficiency Committee was appointed year by year, and they brought far-reaching recommendations for improving the financial plan of the Convention, including the use of budgets and systematic giving.

Meanwhile, various state bodies in the South were engaged in similar studies of their own structures. In 1914, for example, Texas Baptists formed an Executive Board to unify and improve the work of their Convention. This kind of state activity was a part of the Southern Convention's decision to form an Executive Committee in 1917, whose duties initially included recommending ways for a "steadier and more dependable stream of contributions" for missions.

Another important factor leading to the Cooperative Program was the Seventy-Five Million Campaign. This was a joint effort by the Convention and the state bodies to raise $75,000,000 in the five-year period from 1919 to 1924, all receipts from which would be divided equally between the Southern Convention and the state bodies. The early success of the movement was encouraging, as advance pledges totaled over $92,000,000. Both state and convention agencies anticipated receiving no less than the amounts to be allocated to them from the total goal, so they promptly enlarged their benevolent programs accordingly, borrowing funds in anticipation of receipts. However, the depression following World War I began to grip the rural areas of the South early in the 1920s. Since most Southern Baptist churches were rural, they were quickly victims of the depression. As a result, only $58,591,713 was raised in the five-year period, leaving Baptist state bodies and the Southern Baptist Convention deeply in debt.

In 1923 a Committee on Future Program was named by the Southern Baptist Convention to make plans for Convention goals after the close of the campaign. This committee included the heads of the Convention boards, the presidents of the three seminaries, representatives of the Woman's Missionary Union, state leaders, and other outstanding southwide members. It was a good thing that this committee possessed such excellent personnel, for in addition to the critical financial situation, Southern Baptists were in the midst of stormy times. J. Frank Norris and his followers were challenging the Convention and its agencies on their attitude toward the evolutionary hypothesis of Charles Darwin and its theological implications. At the very time the Convention was meeting at Memphis in 1925, the famous Scopes trial in the same state involving this question was being widely discussed. As a matter of fact, the entire nation was in political, moral, and economic turmoil. The revelations of the Teapot Dome scandal rocked even the moral insensibilities of the "Roaring Twenties." The worst financial collapse in American history was imminent, to be followed by the longest and most severe depression this nation has ever known.

In this context the Committee on Future Program made its definitive report to the Convention in 1925. It reiterated previous recommendations that each Southern Baptist church adopt an annual budget which would include undesignated gifts for local, state, and Convention-wide denominational work and that each member be urged to make a pledge to this church budget through a simultaneous every-member canvas.

But the committee's recommendations went beyond that. Remembering the impressive cooperation between the state bodies and the Convention in the Seventy-Five Million Campaign, it proposed that a large and representative commission be appointed, including leaders from both Baptist state bodies and the Southern Baptist Convention, which would be known as the Commission on the Cooperative Program. This commission would spearhead a new plan of formal cooperation between the state bodies and the Southern Convention. These recommendations were adopted by the Convention in 1925 with the concurrence of state leadership.

When we talk about the Cooperative Program today, it is this remarkable plan of cooperation between the individual Baptists, the churches, the state bodies, and the Southern Baptist Convention that occupies the forefront, although the other significant parts of the program made this a single package. In 1979, for example, the *Annual* of the Southern Baptist Convention defined the Cooperative Program as follows:

> The Cooperative Program is a financial channel of cooperation between the state conventions and the Southern Baptist Convention which makes it possible for all persons making undesignated gifts through their churches to support the missionary, education, and benevolent work in their own state convention and also the work of the Southern Baptist Convention.

How the Cooperative Program Works

The inauguration of the Cooperative Program in 1925 represented a radical change in every area of Baptist financial practices. Individual Baptists and local churches were affected. Formerly a missionary speaker would bring a stirring message from the pulpit on the particular benevolence he represented and take an offering for the work. Few churches had budgets or goals for mission offerings, so the mission board had no information in advance about the success of the "roundup" in the fall or in the spring. Their work had to go on, so it became a practice for the boards to borrow money from banks until offerings came in. They hoped the offerings would equal the amount of the bank loans plus interest.

With the adoption of the Cooperative Program in 1925, however, in a remarkable example of wise leadership and grass-roots loyalty, Southern Baptists began making pledges to their church budgets and bringing their tithes and offerings week by week. Church budgets were subscribed in advance and provided support for state and world missions to be sent to the state office each month. This pattern united each pastor with all the missionary and benevolent work of the denomination in a new way and made him a champion of denominational work, state and southwide.

State conventions also experienced changes in methodology after 1925. Formerly speakers from the various southwide agencies would appeal for designated funds from the platform. Under the old plan state conventions could designate some of their members as messengers to the Southern Baptist Convention for funds provided in their offerings. A new pattern began in 1925. State bodies prepared financial budgets for the following year to include not only funds for the work in their own state but also to promote undesignated gifts for the Conventions's missionary and benevolent programs. Each state determined what percentage of their total undesignated funds would be forwarded to the Southern Baptist Convention each month. Some state bodies sent 50 percent, others, 40 percent, or whatever percent was voted by their constituency.

The Southern Baptist Convention also had some adjustments to make, and happy adjustments they were. As the Cooperative Program now operates, each agency of the Convention submits its financial needs to the Executive Committee well in advance of the budget year. The Executive Committee prepares several overall budgets for presentation to the Convention for approval. The first budget includes the basic operating needs for the minimal work of each agency. If undesignated gifts exceed the minimal budget, a second budget provides amounts for capital needs as identified by each agency. A third budget includes funds for supplementary needs for each agency if funds are available. If money remains for distribution, a final allocation is provided on a percentage basis. In 1985, for example, the final allocation was divided as follows: 50 per cent for the Foreign Mission Board; 20 per cent for the Home Mission Board; 15 percent for the six seminaries; and 15 percent for the Radio and Television Commission. The old plan of employing agents to seek designated funds was discontinued. The people, the pastors, the churches, and the state bodies made a remarkably rapid adjustment to the new plan, and Southern Baptists moved into a new and brighter day.

In this program, every Baptist principle of freedom and autonomy is safeguarded. If any member of a church is unwilling to follow the budget adopted by his church, he may eliminate any items by designating his gifts. This is true with gifts by the church to the state bodies and the Southern Baptist Convention. The final choice rests with the conscience of the steward. He should recognize, of course, that under the present structure, designated gifts to the local church, the state bodies, and the national Convention are taken into consideration in making up the budgets, and if the majority votes to provide funds for any program, the ultimate result will be a readjustment of budgets to carry out the will of the majority.

Criticisms of the Cooperative Program

Of course, the Cooperative Program has been criticized for several reasons. Some of these are obvious.

Money and Finances

First, the Cooperative Program functions in a very sensitive area of life: money and finances. The nature of money makes this true. Money is a chunk of ourselves in concentrated form. We accumulate it generally by investing our time, talents, and energy; it represents a portion of our lives. When we give our money for any purpose, we are actually giving a part of our lives. This is one of the reasons Christians who cannot go to the uttermost parts of the earth are sensitive to missionary needs and give their money as a part of carrying out the Great Commission: They are going through their gifts.

The Scriptures say a great deal about money. Our Lord taught that money accurately reflects our priorities in life. After urging His disciples to lay up treasures in heaven rather than on earth where moth and rust corrupt and thieves steal, He said, "For where your treasure is, there will be your heart be also" (Matt. 6:19-21). He also taught that the proper use of our money involved an enlightened stewardship. In the parable of the talents, our Lord described the action of an unenlightened steward who simply hid his lord's money when he could have at least received interest on it (Matt. 25:24-28). Faithfulness is basic in a proper stewardship (1 Cor. 4:2). Money should reflect our proper relationship to others, for we should not bring a gift to God until we are reconciled to our brother (Matt. 5:23-24).

Some of the earliest opposition to mission work in American Baptist life stemmed from the constant appeals for money. Especially on the frontier where money was a scarce item, men like John Taylor and Daniel Parker expressed their utter contempt for these missionary "money-mongers" who preyed upon unsuspecting people.

A Question of Control

A second reason for criticism of the Cooperative Program has been the historic Baptist attitude that money is a means of ecclesiastical control. Rightly or wrongly, Baptists have always used money in religious politicking. In the earlier days of American Baptist life, the most popular way to get rid of a pastor was to "starve him out." If the pastor's sermons were too short or too long, if he attacked the wrong evils from the pulpit, if he were not interesting enough to command large crowds, if he did not visit, if he had any worrisome habits, or if he were not a likable person, the first sign that he would not remain long as pastor was the dramatic decrease in offerings for his support.

This use of money as a means of control extended to denominational life. Baptists chose the financial basis rather than the denominational basis for organizing their earliest general bodies. In the history of the three Baptist benevolent societies between 1814 and 1845, there are many examples of groups withholding their funds from the societies if some action by the society aroused the ire of its constituents. There is evidence that this idea of control was involved in the adoption of the society pattern of designated giving by the Southern Baptist Convention when it was formed in 1845.

Other Appeals for Support

The Cooperative Program has become less appealing because of the rapidly increasing flood of appeals for support from every part of the nation. Electronic churches spend a great deal of their television time asking for funds. Some large churches major on their radio and television ministry, some of it quite expensive, to extend their influence. Numerous charitable organizations now appeal directly to the public through radio and television to finance specific programs, such as food for starving children in foreign lands and research for various diseases like diabetes or cystic fibrosis. The very quantity of these and other appeals has tempted some Baptists to use some of their resources for these objects.

For these and other reasons, criticisms of the Cooperative Program have appeared in "Letters to the Editor" in many

Baptist papers, in Baptist articles published in periodicals, and in editorial comments in various Baptist papers.

As an example, some critics have argued that a strong television ministry by a church was a much better investment of tithes and offerings than undesignated gifts to the Cooperative Program. This criticism reflects a lack of information about the value of the Cooperative Program for Southern Baptists. It can probably be answered only by redoubling our efforts to inform all of our people of the central place the Cooperative Program plays in the life of Southern Baptists.

Lack of Motivation

Another criticism has asserted that the Cooperative Program does not motivate people to want to give it wholeheartedly support. There may be some grounds for this criticism. While responsible and dedicated leaders are bending every effort to inform Baptists of the magnificent work supported by the program, the ministries of our denomination have become so numerous and diverse that it is difficult to communicate the whole story of any one particular aspect. But the fundamental nature of the achievements of the Cooperative Program needs to be projected to our people regularly and dramatically.

Our participation needs to be more than providing one section in the budget. The reports of undesignated funds must be transformed into moving accounts of victories for our Lord on some distant mission field, the ministry of a hospital and its Christian witness in India, the evangelistic efforts among people in Africa, or the unbelievable transformation wrought by the gospel message in some slum area of an American city. Our pastors need to use illustrations from our mission fields to remind the people of the ministry of their undesignated dollars.

Our literature must break down statistics into individual examples of the challenges and achievements of those utilizing Cooperative Program dollars. For example, during most of the nineteenth century the reports of the several agencies, especially the mission boards in the *Annuals* of the Convention, consisted principally of stories and letters from different areas of their work. With the extensive growth of the Convention, it has become necessary to frame these reports in statistical form describing the attainment of objectives during the previous year. Much of the inspirational content of these reports has been sacrificed to the necessity of concentrated summaries. We must find other ways to paint pictures and tell stories which show the work of our Cooperative Program.

Sometimes controversies lower our motivation to participate in the Cooperative Program. While Baptists must always guard the freedom to speak their minds, we must also take care lest we harm the Cooperative Program, the most successful and efficient method of mission funding in history.

The Excellencies of the Cooperative Program

Let us turn from these criticisms to summarize briefly some of the contributions of the Cooperative Program. The Cooperative Program has now existed for over sixty years. It has been refined in its form, but basically it is the same plan that was adopted in 1925. In 1985 it provided $309,798,124 in undesignated funds for state and worldwide ministries; the Convention received $117,526,691 of that amount. It has proved to be of incalculable value for Southern Baptists.

Organizational Consistency

First, the Cooperative Program has helped bring an organizational consistency to the Southern Baptist Convention for the first time in its history. From an organizational standpoint, it is unthinkable to consider returning to the antidenominational society pattern of designated giving which was practiced before 1925.

The financial needs of our present Convention cannot possibly be met by a program of designated giving. Rivalry for funds, the multiplication of agents to promote each object of the Convention, the dilemma of the pastor who is asked to allow appeals for designated funds from his pulpit almost every Sunday of the year, and numerous other major problems would develop if we returned to the old society pattern. To bring back the organizational ambivalence that mingled denominational and antidenominational elements, as the hybrid Convention operated before the elimination of the society elements, would wreak havoc in every part of our denomination as we know it today.

Unifying Nature

A second excellence of the Cooperative Program has been its unifying nature. Never before has the ideal of the Convention's founders been so visible in "eliciting, combining and directing the energies of the whole denomination in one sacred effort for the propagation of the gospel." The joint efforts of the state bodies and the Southern Baptist Convention to meet the challenge of the gospel for the whole world mark a new day in the history of Southern Baptists.

The voluntary nature of this cooperation is evident at every point. The individual is free in making his pledge to the church budget, the church is free in making its undesignated gifts to the state body, and the state organization is free to send whatever percentage it will to the Southern Baptist Convention for world missions. Yet all are bound together by the charge that is upon them from the commissions of our living Christ. This formal cooperation between the state and national bodies has united churches, pastors, and the denomination in a way Southern Baptists had never before known by replacing the agents who solicited designated gifts before 1925 with pastors who strive to advance every part of the denominational effort to reach the world for Christ.

Scriptural Financial Methodology

Third, the Cooperative Program has brought Southern Baptists to a scriptural financial methodology. The necessity for a continuous and systematic expression of our stewardship is taught by the Scriptures. In Luke 12:41-48 Jesus reminded His disciples of this truth in the story of the imminent return of the Bridegroom and the need that wise and faithful stewards be busy carrying out their stewardship when He returns. He then said to His disciples, "Be ye therefore ready also: for the Son of man cometh at an hour when ye think not" (v. 40). In 1 Corinthians 16:2 Paul said, "Upon the first day of the week let every one of you lay by him in store, as God hath prospered him, that there be no gatherings when I come." In 1 Peter 4:10 the apostle exhorted, Be "good stewards of the manifold grace of God."

This continuous and systematic expression of our stewardship is a significant part of the Cooperative Program that is often overlooked. Before 1925 this concept of Christian stewardship was minimized. Regardless of the need for the gift, the need to give is an imperative of the Christian life. For most of us, our gifts to missions will be the only way we have to obey the commission of Christ to go to the uttermost parts of the earth.

The Cooperative Program emphasizes the need to bring our offering for world missions week by week as God has prospered us. This becomes an aid to worship as we are constantly reminded of God's ownership and our stewardship. The burden of a lost world is faced each week as we make our gifts. This scriptural practice also provides the opportunity of regular training for the young people in our homes and churches. Training of a future generation in biblical stewardship is an added blessing to the fulfillment of our stewardship and the meeting of the needs of a lost world.

Financing the Work of God

Fourth, the Cooperative Program has proved itself to be an effective and efficient method of financing the work of God. Our missionary leaders have called the Cooperative Program the "lifeline of missions." Statistics are sometimes deceiving, but they do provide one method of evaluation. Mission gifts of Southern Baptists increased from $8,255,435 in 1925, when the Cooperative Program was inaugurated, to $610,668,080 in 1985. This rate of increase far outstrips inflation and the rate of growth of the constituency. Another relevant statistic is the increase of the receipts of the churches. These have grown from $1,513,640 in 1925 to $3,886,048,305 in 1985. Undesignated gifts increased from none in 1925 to over $300,000,000 in 1985. This undesignated sum has made it possible for Southern Baptists to add many adjunctive ministries by both the state bodies and the Southern Baptist Convention which would not have been supported under a program of financial designation.

Some have raised the question of the efficiency of the Cooperative Program in carrying out its vast ministries. Occasionally someone will say, "I designate my gifts so that all of it goes to the object of support and none to administration." This kind of statement is not based upon the facts, for every agency has administrative costs, whether it is an independent society dealing with only one benevolence like foreign missions or a small denominational body with a great deal of voluntary service. The fact is that the Cooperative Program's administrative cost averages from 2 to 4 percent. It is unlikely that any organization of any kind has a more efficient operation.

Planning in Advance

Fifth, the Cooperative Program made it possible to utilize advanced planning to great advantage. Advanced budgeting and monthly receipts enable our leaders to monitor carefully the nation's economic climate month by month. Monthly disbursements provide adequate budget controls on a short-term basis. A drop in receipts provides warning flags and permits early adjustment of budgets. The expensive and embarrassing practice of borrowing funds for current operations has been eliminated. This kind of advanced planning has led to a number of other refinements in the operation of the Convention and in supervising the functions of each agency.

The Convention, in addition, has provided for each agency to accumulate a reserve fund for use in financial emergencies. During the severe depression of the 1930s, some of the missionaries of independent societies and denominations without stabilizing boards found themselves stranded on the foreign field without sufficient funds to buy food or to pay their fares back to the United States. Our Southern Baptist missionaries came to the aid of several in this situation at that time. The knowledge that our denomination provides emergency resources because of its love and concern for them helps our missionaries devote themselves to the pressing tasks facing them.

Trust and Confidence

Sixth, the Cooperative Program has encouraged trust and confidence. Millions of Southern Baptists have never attended a Southern Baptist Convention's annual session to vote on the distribution of funds. Yet these millions trust the judgment and integrity of their leaders in disbursing carefully the funds which all Southern Baptists have provided. Trust is a much-needed commodity among Southern Baptists in all of their dealings.

Baptist Responsibility

Finally, the Cooperative Program has magnified our corporate Baptist responsibility. Individuals may bring their tithes and offerings to their churches, and under the Cooperative Program the churches and state bodies have learned to share their undesignated gifts in the worldwide ministries of the Southern Baptist Convention.

In conclusion, the Cooperative Program is not some sort of sacred cow that requires no constant care and supervision. Any structure for financial cooperation would require this. Voluntary cooperation must be able to accept diversity and freedom while inculcating loyalty and responsibility. The value of the Cooperative Program can best be glimpsed by comparing its results with the tensions and ineffectiveness of the financial methods used before 1925. From a structural standpoint, Southern Baptists experienced one of their finest hours in the days of crisis of 1925 when they developed the Cooperative Program. As the Executive Committee remarked in 1939:

> It was slow and gradual in its formation. It arose out of the desires and efforts of pastors and churches to find a plan whereby all worthy denominational causes might be cared for fully and fairly without conflicting with the necessary progress and work in the churches themselves. It is believed to be sane, scriptural, comprehensive, unifying, equitable, economical and thoroughly workable.

THE SOUTHERN BAPTIST CONVENTION Executive Committee disburses Cooperative Program funds according to the budget approved by SBC messengers. Some 20 boards and agencies receive Cooperative Program funds.

- Home Missions 20%
- Seminaries 20%
- Foreign Missions 50%
- Other 10%

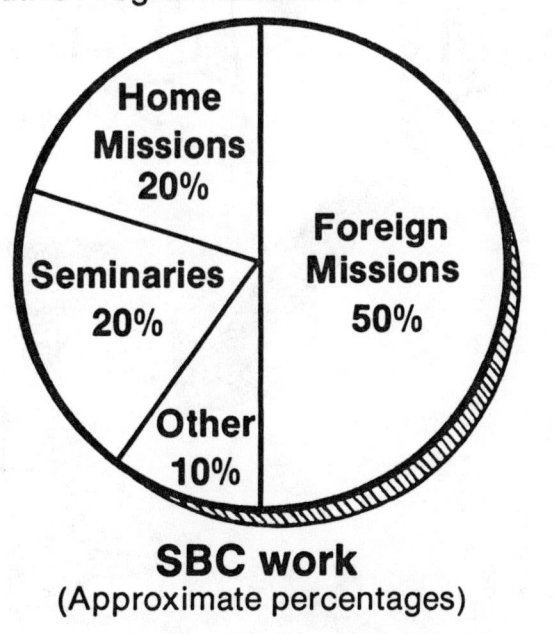

SBC work
(Approximate percentages)

Churches cooperate through associations, state conventions, and the Southern Baptist Convention. Each of these entities is autonomous but interdependent.

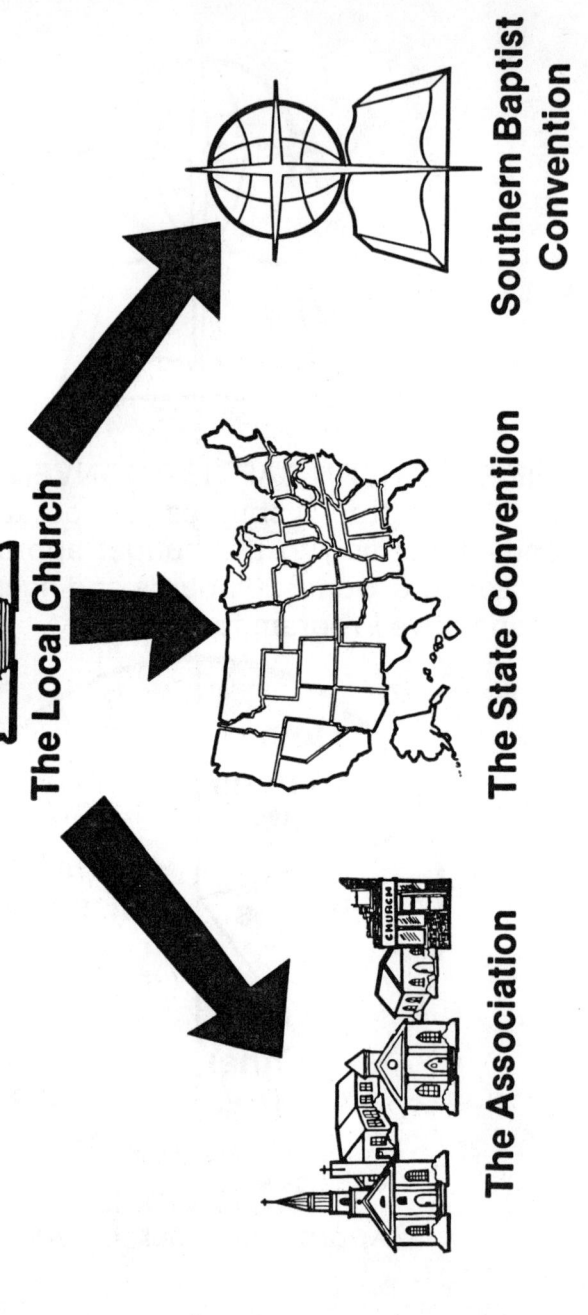

The Local Church

The Association

The State Convention

Southern Baptist Convention

Part II
The Local Church and the Cooperative Program
Daniel G. Vestal, Jr.

4

The Church as a Base for World Missions

Rediscovering the Gospel

I love being a pastor, and I love participating in the worldwide expansion of the kingdom of God as pastor in a local church. Though I may not be as ambitious as John Wesley who said, "The world is my parish," I do feel compelled to say, "The world is my concern." I am bothered that children are hungry, that families disintegrate, and that people are lost without Christ in places other than where I live. I do care about the gospel being preached and accepted in Bucharest, Rumania or Rio, Brazil, just as I care about the gospel being preached and accepted in Midland, Texas, USA.

For me missions is a passion before it is a program. It is a spirit prior to a structure, a motivating urge more than any method. Missions is a fire burning in my soul. "We cannot but speak the things we have seen and heard" (Acts 4:20). "Daily in the temple, and in every house, they ceased not to teach and preach Jesus Christ" (Acts 5:42). "Therefore they that were scattered abroad went every where preaching the word" (Acts 8:4).

Missions is born out of an inner compulsion. It comes from an insatiable desire to share Jesus Christ with others. C. T. Studd said,

> Some want to live within the sound of church or chapel bell.
> I want to run a rescue shop within a yard of hell.

Why? Because an inward desire captures and compels. Anyone who has ever felt that desire understands. And those who haven't don't.

The challenge of our day demands a recovery of this passion. Nothing can substitute for it. Calculated planning, denominational programs, or frenzied rhetoric will not motivate the church of the Lord Jesus Christ to fulfill the Great Commission. Statistical information or guilt-producing appeals will not mobilize believers for mission. Motivation must come from inward conviction and compulsion.

Where does this motivating urge originate? From where does it come? How does it differ from simple human compassion? Is it only a psychological or emotional impulse? As a pastor I have asked the same questions many other pastors have asked: How are people motivated for missions? What is the handle or the tool that can be used to compel them, to capture them for involvement? I have tried, as I know others have tried, to produce motivation and have failed miserably.

Nothing less than a rediscovery of the gospel itself will bring revival and motivate for mission. And that discovery must be more than either intellectual or emotional. It must penetrate to the very depths of our spirit. Therein is the miracle.

Each person's conversion and pilgrimage is unique. For me it has been more of a process than an experience, although memorable mountain peaks, valleys, and crossroads have characterized the journey. From my earliest consciousness I have desired the gospel. Even before I understood it, I wanted it. After hearing it and accepting it, I have loved it the more. I was much like the music teacher who said of her music students, "My students love music. They eat and sleep and breathe music. I just wish they could read music."

I was reared in the home of a vocational evangelist and was attracted to the gospel at a young age. I was attracted not only to the gospel but also the task of spreading it. Somehow I felt from the very beginning that the good news was not my own private possession and that I *must* be about the business of communicating it, sharing it, and telling it.

Perhaps in those earliest years, my father's fervor warmed my own soul. Perhaps the missionary vision of my home church nurtured me. Perhaps an early exposure to the excitement and intensity of revival evangelism influenced me. However the factors worked together, early in my life I learned a love for the Lord Jesus Christ and for the responsibility of telling others about Him. That early love has since blossomed into a romance, and it is a great part of the missionary motivation for my ministry as a pastor.

> I love to tell the story Of unseen things above,
> Of Jesus and his glory, Of Jesus and his love:
> I love to tell the story Because I know 'tis true;
> It satisfies my longings As nothing else can do.

I have come to believe that only God can truly motivate His people for mission. One way He does that is by enabling us to see in fresh new ways the wonder of His glorious gospel. He inspires us by allowing us to catch a glimpse of His redemptive purposes in the world. He compels us by giving us insight into His sovereign plan of redemption. He motivates us by quickening our consciences and enlightening our minds so that we can understand, believe, and be excited about the gospel.

Rediscovering the Responsibility of the Gospel

"I am debtor both to the Greeks, and to the Barbarians" (Rom. 1:14).

Motivation for missions is woven into the fabric of the gospel because missions is woven into the fabric of the gospel. Therefore, a rediscovery of the gospel will result in a rediscovery of the responsibility inherent in the gospel. This will mean an inner compulsion not only to accept Jesus Christ but also to share Him.

What is the gospel anyway? It is the good news that God

loves us in spite of our sin and sent His only begotten Son, Jesus Christ, to be our Savior. As we repent of sin and trust God's Son, our lives are brought under His lordship; we are enabled to love Him, follow Him, and serve Him. In so doing we become part of God's redemptive mission.

Salvation, therefore, is more than an acceptance of Jesus Christ, we participate with Him in His Kingdom. My participation is voluntary but not optional. Eternal life is a relationship with God which brings forgiveness, joy, and peace. But that relationship with God also brings involvement with Him as He reconciles the world to Himself. Jesus Christ died for my sins, but He also died for the sins of the world. If I accept salvation from His death, I must also accept His concern for the world.

Acceptance of the gospel is more than acceptance of a personal, private salvation. To accept the gospel is to become a steward who accepts a trust. The confession of the apostle Paul, "I am debtor both to the Greeks, and to the Barbarians, both to the wise, and to the unwise" conveys a basic understanding of the Gospel that motivates for mission. Implicit in this confession is the conviction that the gospel is entrusted to us. We are stewards of the gospel. We owe it to the world. As long as there is an unsaved person, we are in their debt.

All of us feel gratitude to God for His goodness. "Bless the Lord, O my soul, and forget not all his benefits" (Ps. 103:2). "What shall I render unto the Lord for all his benefits toward me?" (Ps. 116:12). We can understand indebtedness to the Lord Jesus Christ for His atoning death and sacrificial love. "For ye know the grace of our Lord Jesus Christ, that, though he was rich, yet for your sakes he became poor, that ye through his poverty might be rich" (2 Cor. 8:9). We can surely understand indebtedness to friends and family who have loved us, to Christian individuals and churches who have nurtured us. All of us owe so much to so many.

But what motivated the great apostle to the missionary task was an indebtedness to those who had never done anything for him or for God. He saw himself in debt to those who were separated from God, strangers, aliens, even enemies of God. That indebtedness formed a great part of his missionary vision and spirit.

Humanity was on Paul's heart in all the differences of culture. On the one hand, there were "the Greeks" or "the wise." The Greco-Roman culture of Paul's day formed what we would call classical civilization. It was comprised of the thinkers, the cultured, the educated of that day. Unceasingly the apostle-missionary preached the gospel to these people. Whether to Sergius Paulus, a proconsul (Acts 13:7), or to Lydia, the seller of purple (Acts 16:14), or to the philosophers at Athens (Acts 17:18 *ff.*), the apostle faithfully discharged his indebtedness.

We, too, owe the gospel to those of our world who would be classified as educated and cultured. To people in the academic centers, to the technicians and scientists, to the "movers and shakers" of society, we owe the gospel. To the intellectuals and politicians, to the managers and professionals, we owe the gospel. To the communicators and opinion makers of the world, we owe the gospel.

Paul also spoke of "the Barbarians" or the "unwise." These were the people of numberless tribes and tongues whom the educated world forgot or even despised. These were the untrained in schools who knew only work in the fields or markets. To these, as well, the apostle-missionary preached: the Philippian jailer (Acts 16:27), the island inhabitants of Malta (Acts 28:1) and the multitudes in Ephesus (Acts (19:18).

We, too, are indebted to the people in the world who have no wealth, no position, no power. Indeed, the Scripture seems to place a special emphasis on the fact that Jesus preached the good news of the kingdom to the poor, the disfranchised, and the helpless. (Luke 4:18; 7:22) Stern warnings are given about showing preference to the privileged (Jas. 2:2-5; 1 Tim. 5:21). The strong indication is that the majority in the early churches were "common people" (1 Cor. 1:26)

The responsibility of the gospel is that we not only accept it but also share it. In fact, because we accept it, we must share it. "Necessity is laid upon me; yea, woe is unto me, if I preach not the gospel! For if I do this thing willingly, I have a reward: but if against my will, a dispensation of the gospel is committed unto me" (1 Cor. 9:16-17).

Rediscovering the Glory of the Gospel

"I am not ashamed of the gospel of Christ" (Rom. 1:16).

No cause, no controversy, no call is more exciting that that of fulfilling the Great Commission because no story, no message, no truth is more glorious than the gospel of Jesus Christ. In addition to his confession of indebtedness, the apostle Paul offered a ringing affirmation and enthusiastic conviction about the gospel: "For I am not ashamed of the gospel of Christ."

Let's be honest in admitting that there is a shame among us about the gospel. For some there is an intellectual shame. Many people are not sure that the gospel has the essential philosophy and virility of thought to commend it to tough minds. They are cynical about the ability of the gospel to compete in the marketplace of ideas. They are unsure about the relevance of the gospel to the pressing problems of world governments. They are tentative in their conviction that the gospel speaks to the depth and complexity of the human condition.

Other people have a cultural shame about the gospel. When they confront cultures foreign to their own, especially those shaped by strange religions and philosophies, they are offended by the exclusive claim of Jesus Christ, "I am the way, the truth, and the life: no man cometh unto the Father, but by me" (John 14:6). They can readily admit to the Christian gospel being one way among many ways to God, but they stumble at the radical statement, "Neither is there salvation in any other: for there is none other name under heaven given among men, whereby we must be saved" (Acts 4:12).

Still others are socially ashamed of the gospel. They profess belief and adherance, but they are so concerned about the opinions and approval of their peers that they never risk anything to evangelize. The result is that timidity is actually embarrassment. It is shame. More than anyone wants to admit, believers do fear "to own his cause, or blush to speak his name."

In contrast to all of this, the apostle affirmed, "I am not ashamed of the gospel of Christ." He believed the gospel. He loved the gospel. He lived by the gospel. He was captured by it, motivated by it, and willing to die for it. He gloried in the gospel.

Nothing less than that kind of enthusiasm for the gospel will motivate the church of the Lord Jesus Christ for world missions. More than anything else, we need that enthusiasm. More than elaborate programs, more than beautiful buildings, more than modern means of communication, we need a revival of the spirit. We need a revival of the spirit that will ignite within us the same fire for the gospel that Paul had. When it happens the missionary task will become to us the exciting adventure that it is, the glorious passion of our lives, and the triumphant conquest of the kingdom of God.

Rediscovering the Power of the Gospel

"It is the power of God" (Rom. 1:16).

Part of Paul's enthusiasm for the gospel was because he had discovered, experienced, and observed its power. The Greek word for *power* is *dunamis*. Our word *dynamite* is a derivative, and it conveys the explosive dynamic and sheer power of the gospel.

The gospel is not just a system of thought or a set of moral principles. It is more than just a world view or pious-sounding phrases. The gospel is power and life. Wherever it is preached and believed, change takes place. Wherever it is accepted and practiced, miracles occur.

The gospel is "the power of God" that changes individuals. Persons can't believe the gospel and stay the same. They must change. They will change. The simple woman who shared a testimony in church is typical of the power of the gospel to change. "I ain't what I ought to be. I ain't what I'm gonna be, but thank God I'm not what I used to be." "Therefore if any man be in Christ, he is a new creature: old things are passed away; behold, all things are become new" (2 Cor. 5:17).

The gospel is "the power of God" that changes families. Belief in the gospel will affect life in the home. Family relationships, attitudes, and practices will take on a different character. A little girl prayed "Dear God, make all the bad people good, and all the good people nice." The gospel has the power to make people both good and nice, beginning in the home.

The gospel is "the power of God" that changes society. The gospel challenges injustice in social structures as well as individuals. The gospel can transform institutions and governments as well as individuals. The gospel can affect culture as well as persons. The gospel has not been tried and found wanting. It has not been tried. But to the degree it is preached, believed, and obeyed in a society, to that degree society will be changed.

Rediscovering the Purpose of the Gospel

"Unto salvation" (Rom. 1:16).

In rediscovering the gospel, we will also rediscover its purpose, salvation. One of the great words of the Bible is *salvation*. It means "rescue or deliverance," and the idea is that God does something for us we can't do for ourselves. Herein is the difference between all other religions and the Christian gospel. Whereas world religions speak of humans doing something for God or doing something for themselves with God's help, the Christian gospel is the glad announcement of

God's doing something for us, in us, and through us that we are incapable of doing. He saves us.

The gospel is the good news that in Jesus Christ God offers us salvation from sin, from condemnation, from darkness, from lostness, and from the judgment to come. The gospel is also the good news that in Jesus Christ we are offered salvation to new life, hope, peace with God, fellowship with God, and knowledge of God.

The gospel means rescue. For me, one of its great truths is that it means rescue from myself. The older I grow, the more I understand sin as self-centeredness and the more I appreciate the purpose of the gospel to deliver me from that to God-centeredness. When I accepted Jesus Christ as Savior, God began working a miracle in me so that I am no longer the center of my life. Christian growth means that by the power of the gospel I decrease, and Jesus Christ increases. His will and glory become more important than my ego and preferences.

Rediscovering the Universality of the Gospel

"To every one that believeth; to the Jew first, and also to the Greek" (Rom. 1:16).

Jesus Christ is either for everyone, or He is for no one. The gospel is either true for the whole world, or it is not true for any part of it. Every human being is born both with the need and capacity to respond to the gospel. It is for "every one that believeth."

Paul's designation "to the Jew first, and also to the Greek" was his way of describing all of humanity. It was his way of pointing out the universality of the gospel. The scope of God's redemptive purpose involves every tribe and tongue, every color and nationality, every language and culture.

We may classify people: Jew and Greek, American or African, Western or Eastern, first world or third world. But with God all such distinctions are superficial. God is gathering unto Himself a people, a church from the uttermost parts of the earth. He has set Himself on a redemptive mission to reconcile the world unto Himself.

Missions is the blessed privilege and awesome responsibility that God gives us to participate with Him in His redemptive mission. His mission will be successful with or without us. The day will come when His kingdom will come on earth as it is in heaven. The day will come when His knowledge will cover the earth like waters that cover the sea.

In sovereign grace and divine wisdom, God has chosen to allow us to participate with Him. He commits to us "the word of reconciliation" and "the ministry of reconciliation." We are allowed to be His ambassadors in the world.

I remember as a boy I learned an old gospel song:

> I am a stranger here, within a foreign land;
> My home is far away, upon a golden strand;
> Ambassador to be of realms beyond the sea,
> I'm here on business for my King.
>
> This is the message that I bring,
> A message angels fain would sing:
> "Oh, be ye reconciled," Thus saith my Lord and King,
> "Oh, be ye reconciled to God."

This is the gospel. And nothing short of a rediscovery of the gospel will motivate and capture the local church of the Lord Jesus Christ for world missions.

Congregational Identity

Nothing can substitute for the local church. I respect missionary and evangelistic institutions that function to spread the gospel and strengthen Christians. I am grateful for small Bible studies and home fellowship groups that meet for evangelism and edification. I rejoice in the budgets and plans of denominational mission boards and other groups interested in missions. But none of these can take the place of local churches. There never has been and never will be a substitute for that visible, functioning fellowship of believers the New Testament calls the church.

I am committed to serving the local church. At times this may not seem as glamorous as having a worldwide itinerant ministry, or being a Christian media celebrity; but as far as I'm concerned, the local church is "where the action is" in extending the kingdom.

What Kind of Church?

As a pastor I have struggled with personal and congregational identity. What kind of church do I want to lead? What kind of church do I want my leadership to produce? Who is the successful pastor? What is a successful church? These questions have far more to do with purpose and character than they do with style or statistics.

Congregational identity is especially important in a day of evangelical resurgence. the persuasive influence of the "electronic church" has created the notion among many that the secret to world evangelism is a Christian broadcasting network, prime time television, or a worldwide communication system. Hundreds of millions of dollars are channeled into media ministries because many sincerely believe that the most significant work of God in today's world is the use of electronics in world missions.

In addition to this, the model of the "superchurch" is held up by many as the successful church. Superchurch is the multistaffed or multiprogrammed church whose budget and programming reflects a commitment to the building of the church as an institution. "Bigger is better," and the criterion for success is usually measurable. Increasingly the superchurch transcends the work of one local congregation and assumes responsibilities formerly thought to be the prerogative of the denomination.

This is surely not the only model a pastor and congregation may adopt in quest for its identity. The charismatic or the neo-Pentecostal movement has created many churches where worship is the cornerstone of church life. Praise, especially in music, is a vital function of the congregation. The pastor functions primarily as worship planner and leader. He is a platform personality, and those who work with him of necessity must also have similar communication skills either in speech, music, or drama.

For other churches the most significant aspect of church life is the pulpit ministry. When one mentions the Metropolitan Tabernacle of London, Charles Spurgeon comes to mind. When one mentions the Crystal Cathedral of California, Robert Shuller comes to mind. Usually what one remembers is the preaching of these men. The priority of the pulpit is obvious, and that priority gives identity to the entire church.

Other models exist for pastors and churches who want to shape their identity. In "the deeper life" church, the pulpit and program focus almost exclusively on living the successful Christian life, the exercise of spiritual gifts, or the fullness of the Holy Spirit. The "denominationally determined" church, looks primarily to the denominational headquarters for calendaring and programming. In the "outreach" church, the number of baptisms and additions is the most important statistic. For the "community action" church, Christian social ministries is the primary concern.

Different models appeal to different pastors, depending on their experiences, training, and temperament. Different models also provide balance in the total body of Christ. Just as no two individuals are identical, no two churches are identical; nor should they be. Geography, needs, and gifts shape the identity of a church. And, of course, the identity of a church can change and can go through passages just as an individual.

Yet with all these considerations and complications, I still am faced with the question of congregational identity. With all the models for church life, I still must struggle with the question, "What will be the purpose and character of my leadership?"

For me the local church is the headquarters for world evangelism. It exists as a base of operation and a system of support for world missions. Its worship, program, and leadership should find its identity in a missionary strategy. The purpose of its very life ought to be to bear witness to its own Jerusalem, Judaea, Samaria, and then to the uttermost part of the earth.

The Church and the Kingdom

The local church is an agent of the kingdom of God; therefore, its identity is tied to the extension of that kingdom. The kingdom of God is a worldwide kingdom that breaks down all human barriers. It knows no racial or geographic boundaries.

The kingdom of God is not confined to any political idealogy, any economic system, or any social structure. It exists in the world, but it transcends time and space. The kingdom has people in it, but the kingdom is not a human institution. The progress of God's kingdom is dependent on human involvement, but the final victory of God's kingdom is not dependent on human involvement.

The local church is to be an embodiment of the kingdom and an instrument of the kingdom. Its methods are to be kingdom oriented. Its message is an announcement and an invitation about the kingdom. Its motives are to be kingdom inspired.

The time has come for pastors to ask the sobering question, "Am I a kingdom person?" The time has come for us to face the issue. "Are we really committed to the kingdom?" Are we more committed to the kingdom than we are to personal interests? There's nothing wrong with a pastor's quest for excellence, aggressive leadership, or the use of promotional skills, but all this must be subordinated to a consuming concern for the kingdom.

We need to be more concerned about the kingdom of Jesus than denominational and institutional loyalties. I owe an unpayable debt to my own denomination and its institutions. But first and foremost I am a follower of Jesus Christ, and whoever else follows Jesus Christ is my brother. Even though we may differ doctrinally, if we acknowledge Jesus as King, we are in His kingdom together. But our denominational churches are not the kingdom. We're servants of the kingdom. We must not identify our churches as the kingdom. The kingdom is much bigger than any of our denominations.

We also need to be more concerned about the kingdom than politics. I love this country and feel stronger every day about patriotism and freedom. But the USA is not the hope of the world, the savior of the world, or the model for the world. The only hope, salvation and model for this world is the kingdom of God.

Focus and Priority

Perhaps the matter of congregational identity is one of focus and priority. Surely no one would deny the importance of multifaceted ministries, electriclike worship, deeper Christian experience, congregational growth, denominational loyalty, and social involvement. But when any one of these (or any combination of these) takes a priority over extension of the kingdom, the identity of a church becomes confused.

When a passion for anything less than the kingdom of God becomes the passion of a pastor and church, they will be considerably less than God intended. When the primary energies of a pastor and church are consumed with anything other than the kingdom, they will in some way become warped and wayward.

The reason missions should have the priority in church life is because the concern of missions is the kingdom of God. The purpose of missions is the reconciliation of the world to God in Christ. The goal of missions is the will of God on earth as it is in heaven.

When a church focuses on missions, it finds an identity that will have balance and strength. Its vision will be as broad as the world, yet as narrow as the next-door neighbor. Its life will be fed by worship, yet it will flow out into active witness and ministry. It will be independently aggressive, yet interdependently cooperative. When extension of the kingdom of God is the focus of a church and when a church loses itself in that focus, it will awaken to an identity that models that kingdom and embodies that kingdom. And when a church loses itself in that kingdom, it will also awaken to an identity that glorifies its King.

5

The Pastor as a Leader in World Missions

A missionary church is a kingdom-oriented church. A missionary pastor is a kingdom-oriented pastor.

Just as the church finds its true identity as it extends the kingdom, the pastor finds his true identity as he leads his church to extend the kingdom. Just as the church is central to God's strategy for extending the kingdom, the pastor is central to God's strategy in leading the church to extend the kingdom.

If as a pastor I am committed to leading the church in extending the kingdom, I will of necessity be committed to world missions. This means then that as a pastor I ought to see myself as a leader in world missions.

I may not be trained in the academic study of missions (missiology), skilled as a strategist or theorist in missions (missiologist), or called to be a career specialist in missions (missionary). Nevertheless I ought to see myself as a significant and strategic leader in world missions. Indeed, my own conviction is that if the church is to succeed in missions the pastor must accept this leadership assignment.

For far too long we have considered the mission enterprise the responsibility of the specialists. We have delegated it to the few. But missions is the task of the whole church. Therefore, leadership in missions must be given by the one who is called to give leadership, the pastor.

How do I as a pastor provide leadership in the world mission enterprise? How do I mobilize and lead one congregation so that it fits into a world strategy for world evangelization? First, I can preach. Second, I can mobilize and equip laypersons for missions. Third, I can lead in stewardship development.

The Pulpit

Gone may be the day when the pulpit was mightier than the throne. But people still want to hear a word from God. They gather week by week with the intent and hope that the messenger behind the pulpit will, indeed, have a divine message of truth and hope.

I find the depth of hunger among God's people for biblical preaching incredible. They don't want to be entertained. Television can do that for them. They don't want to be culturally enlightened or stimulated. The performing arts can accomplish that. They don't want to be politically mobilized. The politicians and journalists can do that. But they do want to be fed. Though there are always those who have "itching ears," a great number of God's people want to be inspired and informed about divine providence and human responsibility. The task and privilege of the pastor is to do just that.

Essential both to God's purposes and human destiny is missions. The pastor, therefore, if he is to be faithful to his call and the gospel, must preach on missions. He must use the pulpit as a mighty weapon in his spiritual arsenal. He must use biblical exposition to confront the church with the divine mandate of missions. He must use history and biography to illustrate the method of missions, and he must use living examples to challenge the church with both the cost and glory of missions.

Mission Preaching Must Be Personal.

If, as Phillip Brooks defined it, preaching is truth through personality, a pastor cannot preach what he is not living. He cannot lead others where he has not been. He cannot proclaim what he does not believe. He cannot preach what he does not practice. A pastor cannot preach missions unless he himself believes it. Mere shibboleths will not do. Lip service will not inspire and motivate people to risk their lives for the sake of the gospel.

Sermons about going and giving will be nothing more than rhetoric if they are not matched by a pastor who goes and gives. Pulpit excellence alone may create admirers, but it won't enlist an army. And what is needed in the mission enterprise is an army of volunteers.

So first of all, mission preaching must be an overflow of a heart for God and the world. Though it may have reasoned logic in it and meticulous exegesis, it must above all else be a compulsion, a call, a conviction.

Too much preaching is theory, unrelated to the life either of the pastor or the people. Particularly is this true of missionary preaching. It is performed rather perfunctorily because of a calendar date, the pressure of a missionary auxiliary, or out of pure duty. This will not do.

A missionary church will not be built apart from a purposeful and persistent commitment on the part of the pastor to preach the missionary message of the Bible. He will not do that until he personally is convicted of the centrality of that message. It must overwhelm him, motivate him, and control him.

A sermon is not a lecture, a speech, or a discourse. It is an event. And the event takes place only when the preacher is both the recipient and conveyer of a message. He is acting, but he is also being acted upon. The Word he proclaims has first been heard by him. It has gripped and confronted him. He has so taken the message to heart that he embodies it. In the moment of proclamation, he is not like a machine sending out a prerecorded message. He is not reciting a memorized lesson.

In the moment of proclamation, the truth the pastor proclaims (always greater than and other than him) has, in a sense, become incarnate in him. You hear his words with your ears, but you hear God's words with your heart. You see and feel his expression and emotion in the delivery, but you sense God's impressions in your spirit. You assimilate in your mind the preacher's logic and reason, but God's directions quicken your conscience.

True preaching, that is worthy of that description, cannot help but be personal. In it the preacher himself is seized by truth. The messenger is overwhelmed by the message. And in that act, he communicates to others.

Missionary Preaching Must Be Positive.

Guilt-producing oratory may produce momentary response, but it will not produce lasting results. Strict allegiance to duty often results in heroic action that inspires, but such inspiration has a way of waning in the face of the harsh realities of life.

Preaching must be more than this. It must capture by surprise, create wonder, and cause excitement. Missionary preaching must appeal to the highest and best that is in us. It must cause us to want to pray, to give, and to go. When it is effective, missionary preaching compels us by attracting us and invigorating us. We are made to feel a sense of privilege when we respond to God's awesome challenge. We rejoice at the opportunity. We gladly give of whatever we have to further the kingdom. We are caught up in a great movement of history. We count everything as loss in comparison to this high call of God.

This is not a mere emotional response (although no Holy Spirit-inspired response is a "mere" anything). It is a glad acceptance of God's way. It is an uncalculating abandon to Jesus Christ. It is a spontaneous and free embrace of the impossible yet certain victory of the cross.

To be sure, the Word of God is bad news before it is good news. The gospel begins with the dark side of the lostness and hopelessness of a world without Christ. We must repent before we enjoy God's grace. We must understand judgment if we are to appreciate forgiveness. The depth of human depravity and suffering must not be ignored. Surely we must weep and mourn. There is a place for sober analysis, and surely there is a need for agony and travail of soul. But I am convinced that the deepest understanding of these realities are grasped in contradistinction to the glorious privilege of participating with God in His worldwide redemptive purposes.

The "great souled" men and women who have made the greatest mark in world evangelism have been those whose love and joy was profoundly simple and simply profound. They served and suffered, they worked and witnessed because the love of Christ constrained them. They went forth gladly and served triumphantly. Missionary preaching calls for this kind of obedience. It believes that such obedience is possible and that only such obedience will sustain missionary zeal.

In spite of the obvious and overwhelming circumstances, and in spite of all odds, missionary obedience is founded on the sure foundation of God's certain triumph. So we who preach, must do so with confidence and hope. We must do so with that same sense of privilege and joy that we want others to have.

Frankly, I have heard many missionary sermons that were depressing. They were depressing not because they aimed at creating sober reflection or honest confession. ("Godly sorrow worketh repentance.") They were depressing because they were hopeless. They gave no way out. The only response that seemed appropriate was to despair, to quit, or to die.

I am not saying that at times we don't need to be brought to our wits' end. We do. But if I understand the gospel, it means good news. Missionary preaching, even in a desperate and decadent world, is good news.

Missionary Preaching Must be Practical.

Oftentimes preaching is not pointed. I am reminded of the lady who asked her minister after a very stirring sermon, "Just what is it you want me to do?" Of course, she should have asked that question of God, but perhaps the preacher could have helped her in her struggle with a more pointed application.

Much missionary preaching is hazy and uncertain. People who hear us preach don't know whether they should pack up and move to Africa, sell everything and give it to missions, or go home feeling miserable. Any one of these responses might be God's will for a certain individual, but perhaps (just perhaps) none of them is God's will. If God's leadership of peoples' lives is an unfolding process and their understanding of His will is a step-by-step experience, then at times, they need specific instruction for the next step.

Preaching in general, and missionary preaching in particular, ought to aim at helping people know the next steps. It ought to be designed with the confidence that some positive response will be made. When that happens, people need to know what to do as well as what not to do.

When young Samuel said, "Speak, Lord; for thy servant heareth," God gave instructions (3:9). When Saul of Tarsus prayed, "Lord, what wilt thou have me to do?" God gave instructions (Acts 9:6). When Isaiah cried, "Here am I; send me," God gave instructions (6:8). *God* gave instructions, and preachers certainly should not usurp God's place. But if preachers are God's messengers, they ought to preach in a way that enlightens. Their preaching ought to help in interpreting the will of God. In leaving worship, believers ought to be able to say, "This I ought to do; this I can do; this I will do."

Missionary preaching ought to be realistic. Expectations ought to be high, but they shouldn't be foolish. There is a difference between faith and presumption. We who preach must be careful that we don't ask of people what even God doesn't ask. God doesn't ask that we bear the weight of the world on our shoulders, bring in the kingdom by our zeal, or finance the expansion of the church by ourselves. So the missionary preacher must not ask that either.

Missionary preaching ought also to be specific. Although the missionary task is as broad as the scope of the gospel and the missionary message is woven into every strand of biblical doctrine, missionary preaching needs to call for specific responses. Not everyone will respond to those specific calls, but some will. Indeed, not everyone should respond, but some must and will.

Apply the mission challenge by calling for a lifetime commitment to vocational missions at one point and by calling for a lay involvement in short-term service at another point. Ask for a sacrificial gift to a mission offering. Ask for a specified period of intercessory prayer in a given time frame. Ask for a specific commitment to a mission project, a mission goal, or a mission strategy. Ask for a personal life-style that would enable mission giving. Ask for a family's involvement in a mission cause. Ask for disciplined praying and learning from youth. Ask for estate giving and will planning in the cause of missions. Ask for a commitment to the ministry of encouragement to missionaries, the ministry of education about missionaries, or the ministry of intercession for missionaries. Be specific.

The Power of Mission Preaching

In 1792 William Carey preached what is perhaps the greatest and most important missionary message in the history of Western Christendom. At the annual meeting of the Nottingham Baptist Association he preached from Isaiah 54:2-3. The theme of the sermon was "Expect great things from God; attempt great things for God." At the end of that message he made an impassioned appeal for a resolution to form a missionary society.

As a result of that sermon and appeal such a resolution was passed, and shortly thereafter, the English Baptist Missionary

Society was born with twelve members. The modern missions movement was launched from a pulpit.

Never underestimate the power of your pulpit. And never underestimate the power of your pulpit in mobilizing God's people in the pews for mission.

The Pew

As important as the pulpit may be, the mightiest human resource for world evangelism is not in the pulpit but in the pew. The key to proclaiming the gospel of the kingdom to the nations is the mobilization of the laity. The unharnessed power and reservoir of energy in the pew is staggering. The role of the pastor is to help unleash that power and aid in the release of that energy.

The pastor is called to be an equipper, a teacher, a servant. He is not to be the star on the team but the coach. His greatest effectiveness can be measured not by what he does but by what he trains others to do. He is to be a discipler and a discipler of disciplers.

Especially is this true in world missions. The finest compliment that could be paid a pastor would be that the members of the church are witnessing and ministering to the world, that they are the leaders in evangelism, and that they are carrying the gospel to places the pastor would never be able to go.

Perhaps this is the place pastors fail most miserably. We often preach earnestly, but we do not equip our lay people for missions. We plead and exhort, but we do little to provide real handles for personal involvement. And if we do, we do it at a distance. Nothing can motivate like the personal participation of a pastor with his lay people in the mission enterprise. Nothing encourages and supports like a pastor calling his people to commitment and then responding to that call himself and being a volunteer alongside them.

Many lay people are responding to the mission challenge by asking, "How?" Part of the pastor's role is to answer that question. Part of the answer lies in his own personal example.

The pastor must be informed and educated about world events, mission strategies, and human need. He must be a learner about career missionaries and complex mission problems so he can pray intelligently. He must know the mission working of his own denomination and how it interfaces with other mission boards and agencies. He must be a reader of mission journals and periodicals. He must take the time to go to seminars, conferences, and workshops on missions.

The pastor must also be a doer, a participant in mission ventures. He must get hands-on experience from witnessing both at home and in mission points. He must cross cultures and barriers to preach the gospel. He must risk and even fail in mission ministries. (This will make him far less critical and far more supportive to others who try and fail.)

To equip laypersons in missions, the pastor must take the mission enterprise seriously enough to do it himself. He must show by his own attempts that missions can't be delegated anymore than prayer can be delegated. It is personal.

Ask Laypersons for Personal Participation.

From a perspective of personal involvement, the pastor must ask laypersons to be involved. Many will respond by saying, "I thought you'd never ask." God has already touched the hearts of some persons who desire more than support roles. Some believers want to be on the front lines of battle, witnessing and working. They may be bored with the tedium of their lives and want the adventure of missions. Some will count it a joy to sacrifice and even suffer. How many will there be? I cannot tell. But if only one person responds, the pastor will find a challenge in supporting and equipping that one.

One word of caution needs to be spoken. Do not ask lay people to volunteer if you are not serious. Nothing is more disillusioning and disheartening to a volunteer than to discover that the call to arms was a false alarm. Nothing will create cynicism like pretend involvement or make-work plans that insult the intelligence and commitment of the layperson.

Count the cost not only for the lay volunteer but also for you when you ask for volunteers.

After the cost is counted and you have some understanding of what is involved, you as the pastor must ask—again and again and again. You must ask with patience and gentleness, with urgency and conviction. Never stop asking. Ask in private and public. Ask the young and the old. Ask men, women, and even children. Ask families and singles. Ask the healthy and the handicapped.

As pastor, you cannot issue a divine call. Only God can and should do that. You must not coerce or pressure, even in the slightest degree. But make clear that missions is everybody's responsibility. Ask each to accept that responsibility.

When you as pastor ask and God as Lord calls, several things will follow. Those who volunteer will realize their need for training and guidance. You will of necessity seek to meet that need.

Accept the Role of a Servant.

To meet the needs of volunteers, the pastor must accept the role of a servant-leader. The servant-leader is different from the master-leader both in attitude and method, and the recovery of servant leadership is one of the keys to the success of a missionary vision in the local church. The willingness of laypersons to be involved personally in missions is an important step, but it is only a first step. They must be equipped.

The equipping task is given specifically to the pastor, and and this simply will not be fulfilled apart from the attitude of a servant. A servant, first of all, has trust. The pastor will need to be secure enough in his own call and identity to trust lay people and to believe that they can do the job. The pastor will have difficulty serving someone without a measure of confidence in those he serves. Trust involves risk, and at times that risk will result in disappointment. But the pastor must be willing to risk and trust the lay people in the mission enterprise.

I cannot emphasize this too much. The pastor must truly believe that the lay people (not just specialists, not just professionals, not just the theologically trained) can make a substantive and significant difference in world evangelization. Though the lay people who step forward for the first time for involvement and training may not be the most talented or gifted, the pastor must show good faith. This is not a call for naiveté or indiscretion, but it is a call for a recovery of radical faith in the power of God to take ordinary persons and do the extraordinary through them. After all, Jesus did exactly this with very unlikely candidates for discipleship and trained them for awesome tasks.

A servant role will also mean that the pastor will lose a measure of control over the mission direction of the church. This is so because laypersons will follow the dictates of their own conscience, which often will leads them in a direction of involvement that the pastor hadn't thought of. The Holy Spirit will quicken and prompt them in what may seem to be a most unlikely direction. Again, the pastor is called upon to trust that prompting and the layperson's ability to understand it correctly.

A pastor must then give time and emotional energy to equipping the laity to do as God has instructed. Such equipping may involve biblical counseling to measure the laypersons' feelings with Holy Scripture. Such equipping may involve detailed guidance in witnessing techniques, sermon preparation, interpersonal relationships, and leadership in worship. Such equipping may involve instruction in prayer and Bible study, church history and doctrine, ethics and psychology.

All this requires a servant spirit from the pastor. For he must train laypersons for tasks he may not have thought of and may not fully agree with. He must give himself to an agenda that he didn't necessarily set and help people achieve goals he didn't determine.

Adopt a Ministry Approach to Missions.

The pastor who wants to be successful in mobilizing those in the pew for world missions must give up his own self. He must die to his own ambitions and desires. He must stop asking, "What do I want for my lay people and church?" and begin asking, "What does God want for my laypeople and church?" Often the answer will not be given to him but to the church. God will speak to them and show them needs they can meet, ways they can witness, and problems they can solve. God will quicken their conscience, stir their spirit, and show them very practical ways they can be involved.

The biblical picture of the church is that it is a body, functioning with different members. Each of us is given gifts. Each of us has a call. And to match those gifts and call, there are needs to be met. I cannot meet the needs that God can use someone else to meet. I cannot heal the hurts, render the help, or minister the love of Christ to everyone, but I can do it to some.

Missions is love incarnated in life. When all of us (pastor or laity) see a hurting, hungry world in rebellion against the holy God and seek to minister the love of Jesus Christ to that world, we will evangelize it. Some of us will do it with the gift of a teacher, others with the gift of a construction worker, a doctor, a homemaker, or an artist. But whatever our gifts or call, we will minister and witness. When we are committed, we will see needs and seek to meet them, using the gifts God has given us.

The Treasury

"Where your treasure is, there will your heart be also" (Matt. 6:21). These words of Jesus give an acid test of Christian commitment. By that test most individual Christians, as well as congregations, would receive very poor grades. The values and priorities of contemporary Christendom in the

Western world reflect a closer tie to secular materialism than to the kingdom of God.

Part of the task of a pastor is to lead God's people in the wise stewardship of material possessions and to lead the church in the wise stewardship of tithes and offerings given through it. The treasury, both in the life of an individual and in a congregation, reflects a theology and a spirituality far more than any rhetoric. Thus a pastor must embody, as well as preach, a personal commitment to Christian stewardship of material possessions. He must be missionary with his own money and lead his congregation to do the same thing.

In order to fulfill our mission, but even more fundamental, in order to be true to the character and destiny of the gospel, we must practice wise stewardship of money. We must be thoroughly Christian in our personal lives and in our congregational life. The remainder of this chapter will be devoted to the subject of personal stewardship. Congregational stewardship is reserved for Chapter 6.

Stewardship Development Must Be Biblically Based.

The authority of all faith and life must be the Bible. This is especially true when it comes to the accumulation, management, and disbursement of possessions. Scripture speaks to the stewardship of life with amazing variety and force.

Serious stewardship development in the church will seek to discover, understand, and apply Scripture; the pastor will teach and train from that perspective. Real growth in missions giving will result from a church's discovering God's will as revealed in Scripture, not just from a fund-raising campaign or an annual pledge drive. We must not be satisfied with anything less than diligent and honest study of Scripture and serious application of Scripture to our lives individually and the corporate life of the church.

What does the Scripture teach about the stewardship of possessions? Scripture teaches that the "earth is the Lord's, and the fulness thereof" (Ps. 24:1), that we are entrusted with a measure of material possessions, and that we will be held accountable for the way we have handled them (Matt. 25:14-30). Scripture teaches that we are to refrain from being slothful or lazy, that we are to work diligently, that we are to be scrupulously and meticulously honest (Rom. 12:17), and that we are to be content and free from greed (1 Tim. 6:8-10; Matt. 6:19).

The Bible teaches the discipline of tithing. It was a law in the Old Testament (Mal. 3:10) and is a standard in the New Testament (Luke 11:42). Tithing provides a divinely ordained pattern for systematic and proportionate giving. The Bible teaches that the followers of Jesus should give according to grace and not in rigid and Pharisaic obedience to the Law (2 Cor. 8:7). A Christian should give according to the example of Jesus who gave sacrificially (2 Cor. 8:9). A Christian should give humbly (Matt. 6:2), purposefully (2 Cor. 9:7), cheerfully (2 Cor. 9:7), and regularly (1 Cor. 16:2). A Christian should give out of desire to meet needs (Acts 4:32-35), out of a commitment of self (2 Cor. 8:5), and out of love for God (2 Cor. 8:8).

Stewardship Must Be Person-Centered.

Stewardship development must be positive and person centered. God's Word will do the convicting and the Holy Spirit will do the changing. But each individual responds to God's Word and God's Spirit in different ways. Our task is to know our people, relate to their weaknesses, answer their questions, and help them learn and grow. I have learned to rejoice in different stages of stewardship development. I have learned to affirm church members who have responded to God's Word and God's Spirit, even though they haven't reached the level of maturity I wish for them.

Don't harangue people. It probably will be counterproductive, and it uses up your energy. Don't ever manipulate people into giving. It may achieve a short-term result, but it will eventually result in disaster. Guilt giving or pressure tactics will not produce cheerful giving. Rigid and legalistic appeals may cause more receipts temporarily but will only set the stage for future difficulties.

Don't be afraid to talk about money, but don't act as though you are an expert. Be an attentive listener, a sympathetic counselor to the financial struggle of your people. Learn to say "I don't know" when faced with a complex financial decision. But move quickly to say, "I will pray with you and search the Scriptures with you as you seek God's will."

Learn to advise and encourage ways of giving and places to give without being authoritative and doctrinaire. Give place to the Holy Spirit as the One who directs God's people, and recognize His sovereignty. Encourage freedom and spontaneity, as well as planning and logic. Don't be greedy for the offerings of your people. When they move beyond the tithe, be willing for them to give to missions and mission causes outside the ministry of your church. Even if you don't get any benefit from their generosity, rejoice in their generosity.

Stewardship development that is person centered recognizes that God is already at work in the lives of His people and seeks simply to be an instrument in God's plan. A person-centered approach will be more concerned about the development and growth of the individual than the church budget and more sensitive to the motive of the person giving than the amount of dollars given.

One of the greatest joys I have received as a pastor has been participating in the awakening of conscience about stewardship in new believers and small children. I remember well a child's stewardship commitment card that found its way to my office one Sunday during a stewardship emphasis. It read, "I pledge to give myself to God and 10¢ a week."

Stewardship Development Must Be Long Range.

Most of us do not grow quickly. Stewardship growth is a process that involves years and even decades. We are slow learners, giving up old ways with reluctance and clinging stubbornly to deeply entrenched patterns of behavior. The man celebrating his ninetieth birthday was greeted by a well wisher with the words, "I bet you've seen a lot of changes in your life," to which he responded, "Yes, and I've been against everyone of them." Growth involves change, and most of us find it difficult to change. Especially is this true when it comes to money.

For this reason stewardship development must take the long look. A pastor must be patient while being doggedly determined to teach and train God's people in wise money management, disciplined tithing, and gracious giving. There are no "quick fixes" or "short-cuts" to stewardship growth. Learning God's ways and practicing God's principles takes time. We are by nature selfish and sinful, requiring God's divine grace and intervening spirit. Growth takes a lifetime.

With this in mind, a pastor ought to preach and teach stewardship on a regular basis. Growth in this area of life is not automatic or easy. God's people need regular instruction, conviction, and inspiration. A pastor must enlist others to teach stewardship who are extensions of his office and those who participate in a ministry of the Word. The whole church needs comprehensive, constructive, and consistent help. Therefore, Sunday School teachers need to give biblical exposition on the subject to all ages—from the cradle to the grave. Training courses ought to be offered periodically to give practical help in stewardship. Literature, tapes, books, and videos can be a forceful ally in a planned approach to training.

A pastor who is faithful in stewardship development may or may not see the results of his labor. He may well plant or water seed that will grow and flower long after his tenure. I can point to several outstanding laypersons in mission stewardship whose present commitment is the result of a church's training decades earlier.

So take the long look. Don't despair if you don't see immediate results. Faithful is He who has called you. God's

Word will not return void. Plan for success in stewardship development, believe God for success, but don't be impatient in demanding that you see all the success.

Biblical instruction on stewardship is much more extensive than this summary. Stewardship development must be from the total context of Scripture. A pastor must seek to be faithful to that context and lead his church in grasping the whole of the biblical message. To lift one aspect of stewardship out of the whole scriptural teaching and isolate it from the rest is to violate Scripture. In other words, the church must develop in tithing and giving as it confronts the whole of Scripture's message on material possessions.

6

Cooperation as the Strategy for World Missions

No matter how effective a pastor is in independently leading his church in mission awareness and involvement, he must do more. No matter how good he is at missionary preaching, missionary mobilization, or missionary stewardship, he must do more. The reason he must do more is because one church alone simply cannot fulfill the missionary mandate. It is impossible. Indeed, it is unbiblical.

Yet some pastors lead and many churches work as if they are the only ones seeking to obey the Great Commission. They may be aggressively evangelistic, but they are narrow in their scope and limited in their mission vision.

A distinction needs to be made between evangelism and missions for the sake of an appeal to partnership in missions. Evangelism is preaching the gospel so that people come to faith in Jesus Christ. It is to be done in the normal traffic pattern of life and as an overflow of love to Christ and love to people. Evangelism is simply sharing Jesus in the ordinary routine of life. It is witnessing to friends and neighbors, as well as strangers in the course of everyday living.

Missions is more than that. Missions is crossing barriers to preach the gospel. Missions is going outside the traffic pattern of our everyday lives for the specific purpose of evangelizing. It's reaching people not like us and people we would not reach if we stayed in our ordinary routine. Missions must be deliberate because the barriers to be crossed are at times awesome. Barriers may be geographical, cultural, linguistic, or social. But missions is the determined commitment to reach across these barriers with the gospel of Jesus Christ. It is a commitment in partnership with others. It is not an isolated or individualistic effort, but an effort made in earnest cooperation with like-minded and like-hearted believers.

Principles of Partnership

The word *partnership* describes the biblical pattern of missions—individuals and churches associating with one another for the purpose of crossing barriers with the gospel. That principle is fundamental to an effective missionary strategy. When believed, it becomes a conviction that will guide a pastor and church as they seek to fulfill the Great Commission.

Voluntary

Partnership must be voluntary. Eternal coercion may produce a uniformity of practice, but it will not produce partnership in missions. Just as individuals must freely choose to respond to God, so must churches freely associate with each other. Partnership must be born out of a desire to achieve the goal that simply cannot be achieved by any one individual or church: world evangelism.

Self-Sacrifice

Partnership requires an element of self-sacrifice. To cooperate one gives up something of self. Personal goals are secondary to goals set together. Listening is as important as speaking. Learning is as important as teaching. Prejudices and presuppositions are challenged. To cooperate one gives up a certain amount of freedom—freedom to publicly criticize, to act judgmentally, or to condescend in attitude. All this requires the grace of God and the power of the Holy Spirit because sacrificing our personal agendas to learn of God's greater agendas is not easy.

Mutual Trust and Respect

Partnership is based on mutual trust and respect. Cooperating to cross barriers for Christ will not mean the erasure of all disagreements (theological or methodological). Indeed, disagreements can be healthy. But essential to cooperation is a common consent to truth. Confidence in one another's motives and integrity is a necessary ingredient to cooperation. Respect for one another's feelings and thoughts is also necessary for cooperation.

Partnership does not mean compromise. In order for Christians to cooperate with one another to extend God's kingdom, we don't have to compromise our convictions or our identity. Nor must churches relinquish their autonomous independence in order to cooperate with other churches. The reason for this is that the basis of our cooperation is the lordship of Jesus Christ. Because Jesus is our Lord, we each follow Him; we each listen to His Spirit; we each obey His Word. In His own beautiful and perfect way, He knits lives together without violating individual identities and responsibilities. Cooperation under the lordship of Christ does not mean compromise. It means unity. It is not a sign of weakness; rather, it is a sign of strength and solidarity.

Commitment and Care

Partnership requires commitment and care. Anything of value takes time and work to develop. Relationships must be nurtured and protected if they are to become life changing. Communication must be open and precise if those relationships are to result in effective mission. Cooperation doesn't happen accidentally. It grows as trust grows.

Participation in Partnership

Cooperative Planning

Cooperative missions requires the time and effort to work together to survey needs, discover resources, and seek God's strategies and methods. Baptists are often accused of spending all their time going to planning meetings. I heard of a woman who said, "I would like to be a Baptist, but I'm not physically able." Someone wrote:

> Mary had a little lamb,
> It was a Baptist sheep.
> It went to all the Baptist meetings
> And died for lack of sleep.

There is the real danger of spending all our time meeting to plan meetings for the purpose of planning still more meetings. We can exhaust our energies in planning and never execute our plans. We can become so organized that we take away the opportunity for spontaneity and actually grieve the Holy Spirit.

But not to plan is also deadly. God can and does guide His people as they dream, plan, and think for the future. He does give wisdom and vision as together they seek to understand worldwide needs and His will to meet those needs. Joint planning need not be cold and calculated logic. It can be energized by the Spirit and enlivened by divine wisdom. It can be exciting. But it needs to be done cooperatively. No person likes to be left out, and very few will have enthusiasm for the plans of another.

Cooperative planning takes concentrated and focused time. It's hard work that requires patience and persistence, but it is highly rewarding. Nothing brings greater joy than participating in a task that is bigger and greater than one individual or one church. Nothing is more rewarding than seeing a seed or a dream grow and blossom into a reality.

Cooperative planning is easiest at the associational level; it becomes progressively more difficult at the state, national, and international level. But at all levels it requires diligence and dedication. It's simply not easy to carve out time from a busy and crowded schedule in a local church to plan, strategize, and dream with churches of like faith and like vision; but it is absolutely necessary.

Cooperative Praying

Perhaps there is no other place where we show whether we are mission minded and kingdom oriented than in how we pray. Most of us pray like the man who said:

> God bless me, my wife;
> John and his;
> Us four, no more.

Most of us are narrow and selfish, even in our praying. We pray only for our needs, our family, our ministry, our church, and our work. If world evangelization is to become a reality, it will require a radical new commitment to world intercession and persistent petition for the kingdom of God to come and the will of God to be done on earth as it is in heaven.

Cooperative prayer for missions is spiritual warfare. Raging in the world today is a great battle—a battle for the minds and souls of people. The battle between the forces of good and the forces of evil is of cosmic proportions. The scope and intensity of the conflict is beyond the comprehension and even the imagination of mortals. At its very center is the Creator—God Himself—and His archrival, the fallen angel Lucifer, Satan, or the devil.

The church is called upon to do battle against this enemy. We actually live in enemy territory and are engaged in this life-and-death struggle. We preach so as to persuade men to leave the kingdom of darkness for the kingdom of light, the kingdom of evil for the kingdom of God.

We will never take prayer seriously in the missionary enterprise until we face the reality of evil in the world and the reality of the evil one in the world. We will never see advance through our missionary efforts if we see missions primarily in terms of promotion, enlistment, organizations, and programs. We must see missions in bigger terms than our institutions or even our churches. We must view missions in terms of a kingdom—the kingdom of God. And if we view missions in terms of extending the kingdom, exalting the kingdom, and entering the kingdom, then we inevitably come face-to-face with the reality of another kingdom—the kingdom of evil. This is spiritual warfare.

What are the weapons of this warfare? As we seek to persuade people for Christ, what are our methods? As we vie with an enemy for the loyalties and allegiances of people, how do we do it? How do we successfully and effectively do battle against our enemy and win the souls of people?

In 1980, I took a group of lay people from our church on a preaching and partnership mission to Bucharest, Rumania. On the last day of that mission, I asked a leading Baptist pastor the secret of Rumanian Christians' spiritual power and vitality. I wanted to know why, in spite of all kinds of opposition, the churches were growing and people were coming to Christ. He answered with these words, "We believe we are in the midst of a spiritual war. And we have discovered that the most powerful weapons for our warfare are the Word of God and prayer." On returning to New York, I took a train to Washington and visited a representative of the National Security Council and also a Rumanian desk officer at the State Department. In the conversation with the career foreign service officer at the State Department, I discovered that he was a Christian. He said to me, "In today's world a spiritual battle rages. And the most effective weapons in this conflict are the Word of God and prayer."

Prayer is a mighty spiritual weapon. When we pray in concert with others, mighty things happen. In some mysterious way when we pray, we release divine energy. When we pray we further the purposes of God and we cooperate with God in the outworking of His divine will. When we pray we literally and actually affect circumstances and people. God works in answer to His people's united prayer.

Cooperative prayer for missions is not just warfare; it is ministry. It is not just preparation for ministry or accompaniment to ministry; it is itself ministry. Prayer is ministry to be performed in the face of great need. After Jesus told the disciples to lift their eyes and see the fields white unto harvest, He told them to pray for laborers (Luke 10:2). After Jesus came down from the mountain of transfiguration and found the disciples unable to help the demon-possessed boy, He told them that some needs are so great that the only form of effective ministry would result from prayer and fasting.

Cooperative prayer for missions is a ministry of love. We will not be able to pray effectively or long endure in prayer for the kingdom unless we care. But if we love, we will pray; in prayer, our love will be intensified. Because I love my wife and children, I pray for them. Because I love the souls of the lost and the kingdom of God, I pray for the mission advance of the church.

Cooperative prayer for missions is a ministry that requires sacrifice and even suffering. If in love I enter into prayer as a form of spiritual service, I will feel a burden of spirit and a heaviness of heart. At times I may weep and agonize. Though prayer is a ministry that requires sacrifice, it is a ministry of great joy. No form of service is more rewarding and thrilling than prayer. Fanny Crosby described the feeling of one who has discovered that joy.

> O the pure delight of a single hour
> That before thy throne I spend;
> When I kneel in pray'r, and with thee, my God,
> I commune as friend with friend!

Cooperative prayer for missions is a ministry that each church must plan for itself. No two churches will do it exactly the same. For many churches prayer is an appendage or on the periphery of an active and busy schedule instead of being at the heart of the church's life. But in the final analysis, a church's prayer ministry for missions cannot be the result of promotion. Rather it is the result of individuals who believe they have a prayer ministry and then dedicate themselves to it.

Cooperative Funding

In its budget a church says more about its commitment to world missions than in any of its rhetoric. How a church spends the money given by the people to God defines its spirit, its theology, and its vision. The disbursement of material possessions is both a reflection of character and an influence on character. That is not only true of individuals and families but also true of churches and denominations.

Why should a church give a high priority to the cooperative funding of world evangelization? What are the factors that should determine a church's percentage to cooperative missions? When should a church put a cap on cooperative giving? And when should a church increase cooperative giving? These are difficult questions to answer, but they must be faced honestly and openly.

First, there is an instinctive and intuitive desire in the hearts of individual Christians and separate congregations to cooperate for missions. Somehow we "feel" and "sense" that we ought to work together even if we can't explain why. An inner impulse and urge to cooperate is natural to us. And if we refuse that impulse, we find it necessary to justify or rationalize why we do.

From where does that cooperative desire come? I believe it comes from God and from the very nature of the gospel. First Corinthians 3:9 says, "We are labourers together with God." That verse has both a horizontal and vertical dimension to it. God allows us to participate with Him in redemptive purposes, and He allows us to cooperate with each other. The essential meaning of the church is that it is a fellowship. The word *fellowship* is the word *koinonia* in the Greek, and that word means "partnership." From the very beginning, partnership involved financial cooperation, as well as other kinds of cooperation. In the early church in Jerusalem, the believers actually had all things in common. In all of Paul's missionary journeys, he collected funds to provide for the suffering saints in Jerusalem. From the earliest pages of the New Testament, churches were concerned about each other's welfare and contributed to each other's welfare. Cooperation is woven into the fabric of God's redemptive plan, and somehow we have a spiritual instinct that responds to that plan.

Another reason for cooperative giving is the overwhelming need and lostness of the world. The mobilization of the church will not only result in individual and congregational witness but also cooperative witness. Cooperative witness inevitably results in institutions that give expression to individual and congregational concern. We must recognize that some concerns need an institutionalized response. Indeed, some needs are so overwhelming that only an institutional response represents a bold response. World hunger, theological education, child care, and the use of media are only a few examples where institutional response is necessary to confront the needs of the world.

Another reason for cooperative giving is the impact and effect it can have on world evangelization. Only God knows how the kingdom would grow if Southern Baptists cooperated financially as Scripture teaches. No longer would there be a shortage of funds to publish literature, support missionaries, buy property, build buildings, and construct radio and television studios. Planning for missionary advancement would be done at a different level, for it would be done with no thought of the contingency of money. We would not worry about how to feed the hungry, clothe the naked, and care for the sick. We would have no problems training and educating leaders, printing enough Bibles, and supporting the necessary ministries of the missionary enterprise.

Although in many ways money is the least of our problems in the missionary task, the lack of it is a symptom of just how serious are our problems. I have always heard, "God's work, done God's way, will not lack God's supply." I believe that. But the fact is that many of God's plans do lack supply because God's people are stingy and selfish. The fact is that we can thwart God's way with our insensitivity, as well as our rebellion.

The resources for world evangelization are available and adequate. God does own "the cattle upon a thousand hills" (Ps. 49:10). But it is also true that Southern Baptists, once mobilized financially, could contribute greatly to fulfilling the Great Commission. We would be amazed if we really knew how much money was spent by Southern Baptists on frivolous and absolutely unnecessary luxuries of life in comparison to how much is given to missions.

More than ever in history, pastors need to give cooperatively and to lead their congregations to give cooperatively. The technology at our disposal, the tools that have been placed in our hands, and the new methods of communication are all gifts of God to be used for world missions. But all these require funding, and what is frightening is that the funding needed could be provided from God's people.

But why the Cooperative Program of Southern Baptists? Why should a church give this priority? Surely this is not the only expression of cooperative missions or cooperative funding in the missionary enterprise. First, the Cooperative Program allows each contributor, both individual and church, the opportunity of a proportionate part in a truly worldwide ministry. Participants are involved in bearing witness to their own Jerusalem, Judaea, Samaria, and then to the uttermost parts of the world. When an individual gives through their church and then that church gives priority to the Cooperative Program, it can be said that the individual's gift will influence the world for Christ. Because of the way Cooperative Program dollars are divided, an individual giver is literally involved in global witness. Very few, if any, expressions of cooperative missions can make this claim.

Also the Cooperative Program allows each contributor, both individual and church, to be a part of many kinds of ministries. The Cooperative Program dollar is divided not only to have an effect geographically in the individual state, the United States, and in countries around the world but also to accomplish tasks of evangelism, discipleship, healing, benevolence, and so forth. The Christian of average income could not possibly be financially involved in so many different kinds of ministries except through a plan like the Cooperative Program. A local church could not make a significant contribution to so many different types of outreach apart from a plan like the Cooperative Program.

Finally, if history has shown us anything, it has shown us that we simply can do more together than we can individually. What is true at a local church level is true at an associational level, state level, and national level. Just as individual Christians accomplish more as they give and work together in the fellowship of the local church, so individual churches can do more as they give and work together in the fellowship of an association or convention. By combining and focusing the resources God has put in our hands, we can be a part of fulfilling the Great Commission.

This has been the overarching vision that has motivated our own church to give high priority to the Cooperative Program. A long-standing conviction that we are to be concerned about the whole world and to seek to win the whole world to Christ has permeated the life and ministry of this church. Through good times and bad, this conviction has persisted and grown. Strong pastoral and lay leadership has been pivotal in deepening that conviction. Perhaps the isolated nature of our environment as a community separated from other communities by miles of open country has increased our awareness of the need for interdependence. Perhaps the pioneer spirit of the West has contributed to a desire to seek to achieve the impossible.

But there is a kind of love affair in our church with cooperative missions. It is an intangible, undefinable dream that one church can make a difference in the world. By cooperating with other churches we can do more than we can individually to fulfill the Great Commission of our risen Lord.

Cooperative Commitment

How does a church make and maintain a commitment to cooperative missions in general and the Cooperative Program in particular? First and foremost, it requires continual education and appreciation for the merits of such an approach to ministry. The more people understand how effective and efficient the mission dollar is when it is channeled through the Cooperative Program, the more likely they will give it high priority. Missions education must be a part of the total educational ministry of a church.

Woman's Missionary Union is an auxiliary to the Southern Baptist Convention, but it must not be an auxiliary to the local congregation. It, like any other ministry of the church, must come under the leadership of the pastor and be incorporated into the total life of the congregation. In our church, the WMU director functions at a staff level, although she is not a paid staff member. She represents the most significant woman's ministry in our church (although there are others) in overall church planning. Woman's Missionary Union, at all age levels, is an invaluable asset in providing information and inspiration about the merits of cooperation. In our church it has been a catalyst in providing literature and leadership in the constant challenge of missions education.

Brotherhood, the mission organization for men and boys, has also been crucial to us in cooperative missions education. It has helped create an environment for men to express their concern and become personally involved in projects and ministries. When they have received firsthand knowledge of how Cooperative Program dollars are spent, when they discover where and how Cooperative Program dollars are spent, they like what they find.

We budget for each church family to receive a weekly copy of our state Baptist paper. This provides information about the workings of the denomination, personalized mission stories, and news about where and how the Cooperative Program works. We invite denominational servants, missionaries, and representatives from agencies supported by the Cooperative Program to speak and share at various church functions. We seek ways and opportunities to inform the fellowship about what and how God is working in His world through Southern Baptists. We encourage participation in the associational, state, and national annual meetings, and we encourage involvement in denominational agencies in our state and nation. This personal involvement results in ambassadors of good will for the Cooperative Program.

Problems in Partnership

Two concerns threaten cooperation as a strategy for world evangelization. The first is a loss of vision. At one time, we as Southern Baptists saw ourselves as a distinct minority. We knew ourselves to be a small band of believers held together by some deep biblical convictions and a common commitment to world missions. From that perspective, we couldn't help but see the lostness of the world and the vastness of the task before us.

Now in many parts of this country, we are part of the social, political, and economic establishment. We have money, status, and position. We have grown significantly in number and have accumulated social status and power. The danger is that we no longer see ourselves as a minority, a called-out company of the committed. The danger is that we no longer see ourselves as a people on mission to a lost and lonely world.

The danger to cooperative missions is that we become enamored with ourselves and expend our accumulated resources on ourselves. I fear we will be more concerned about increasing our status, building our image, and protecting our assets than about the salvation of lost humanity. I fear we will take our eyes off the Lord Jesus Christ and a hungry, hurting world and become preoccupied with ourselves.

In a world of four billion people, we can't afford to have any attitude except that of a servant—a suffering servant—who entirely dependent on God. A danger to cooperation is a loss of vision or an impairment of vision that will lead to a loss of identity and the will necessary to be a mission people. Apathy, indifference, and plain old preoccupation with selfish interests will follow a loss of vision.

A second danger to cooperation as a strategy for world evangelization is the loss of individual responsibility. It is the attitude that says, "It doesn't matter if I pray, somebody will do it. It doesn't matter if I give, somebody will do it. It doesn't matter if I go, somebody will do it." The sad fact in many Southern Baptist circles is that the individual feels lost and unimportant. The individual doesn't feel compelled to take initiative or make a sacrifice. The feeling for many is that the collective ministry can be a substitute for individual ministry.

A young man who had been inspired during a missionary conference went into his pastor's study and said, "I want us to do something big for God." The pastor and young man talked for awhile. The pastor suggested the boy start by taking the names of five unsaved friends and begin to pray for them and witness to them. The young man responded with disappointment, "You don't understand. I want us to do something big for God." He was concerned about cooperative success, but not about individual responsibility.

The great risk in cooperative missions is a slide toward mediocrity. I call it a lull into lukewarmness. It's the attitude that results in everybody's responsibility becoming nobody's responsibility. We must be ever alert and not become smug and satisfied with what we're doing as a group and lose the sense of urgency about what I can do as one person.

In Acts 15:26, a description is given of Barnabas and Paul as "Men that have hazarded their lives for the name of our Lord Jesus Christ." Barnabas and Paul had risked their lives for the extension of the kingdom. They had laid their lives on the line. They had sacrificed so that the gospel of Jesus Christ might be spread. They had paid a price, and they were willing to pay an even greater price for the sake of God's kingdom. Because of them, the mission advance of the early church flourished.

I want to be that kind of man. I want to be that kind of Christian. I don't want it to be said of me that I never personally participated in mission praying, giving, and going. I don't want to be on the sidelines watching while others carry the burden of the kingdom. I want God to use me.

I don't want it to be said that I became so comfortable in my life-style that I was no longer capable of sacrifice. I don't want it said of me that I became so satisfied with collective accomplishments that I no longer felt individual responsibility. I don't want it to be said of me that I became so insulated and isolated from the lost world that I no longer could feel a burden.

> Must I be carried to the skies
> On flow'ry beds of ease,
> While others fought to win the prize,
> And sailed thro' bloody seas?
> ....
> Sure I must fight if I would reign;
> Increase my courage, Lord!
> I'll bear the toil, endure the pain,
> Supported by thy Word.

In the final analysis, world evangelization will take place when each of us says to God, "Here am I, Lord; send me."